F. W. E

Life Verses

The Bible's Impact on Famous Lives

• Volume Five •

kregel
PUBLICATIONS

Grand Rapids, MI 49501

Life Verses: The Bible's Impact on Famous Lives, Vol. Five
by F.W. Boreham.

Published in 1994 by Kregel Publications, a division of
Kregel, Inc., P.O. Box 2607, Grand Rapids, MI 49501.
Kregel Publications provides trusted, biblical publications
for Christian growth and service. Your comments and suggestions are valued.

Cover Design & Artwork: © Tammy Johnson,
                                        Flat River Graphics

Library of Congress Cataloging-in-Publication Data
[A temple of topaz]
Boreham, Frank W. (Frank William), 1871-1959.
   Life verses: The Bible's impact on famous lives, vol.
five / Frank William Boreham.
        p.   cm. (Great text series)
   Originally published: A temple of topaz. London:
Epworth Press, 1928.
   1. Christian biography. 2. Bible—Influence. I. Title.
II. Series: Boreham, F.W. (Frank William), 1871-1959.
Great text series.
BR1702.B63   1994   270'.092—dc20   93-37844
                              [B]   CIP
ISBN 0-8254-2166-7 (paperback)

            1 2 3 4 5 Printing / Year 98 97 96 95 94

Printed in the United States of America

CONTENTS

FOREWORD

When Frank Boreham was four months old, he was on an outing with his nurse when a Gypsy caravan passed by, and an old Gypsy woman, noticing the child, came over to them. She looked at the little boy's hand and said to the nurse, "Tell his mother to put a pen in his hand, and he'll never want for a living." The prophecy proved true. Boreham became one of the world's most prolific religious writers with more than fifty books to his credit, not to speak of hundreds of newspaper and magazine articles and essays.

As the boy grew up, he was introduced to both the things of the Spirit and the things of the mind. Faithful Christian parents saw to it that he was trained in the Word of God and also that he learned to appreciate good reading. Frank's father, noticing that Frank was reading some shallow novels, introduced him to the vast treasures of biography, and the boy was "hooked for life."

In 1891 he united with the Kenyon Baptist Church in Brixton, of which the pastor, James Douglas, was a good friend of C. H. Spurgeon. When the pastor discovered that Boreham was considering the ministry, he naturally urged him to apply to Spurgeon's Pastor's College. Boreham did, and he was the last student that Spurgeon personally selected before his lamented death.

In 1894 Thomas Spurgeon returned to London after ministering in New Zealand, and he brought with him a request for a pastor from a new church at Mosgiel.

The college staff decided that Boreham was their man. He served in Mosgiel, New Zealand; Hobart, Tasmania; and Armadale, Australia; and then he traveled to many lands and preached to vast congregations. Where he was unable to travel personally, his books carried his messages.

The story behind this unique, five-volume series is this: Boreham was about to begin a Sunday evening series when it dawned upon him that a series on alternate Sunday evenings would encourage the congregation to return week after week. As if by inspiration, it came to him to preach on "Texts That Made History." He announced that the next Sunday evening he would preach on "Martin Luther's Text." Little did he realize that these sermons would continue for 125 Sunday evenings and attract more interest and win more people to Christ than any other series he ever preached.

If at first Boreham does not excite you, give him time. He grows on you. He has a way of touching the nerve centers of life and getting to that level of reality that too often we miss. There is something for everybody in a Boreham book because his writing touches on the unchanging essentials of life, not the passing accidentals; we need this emphasis today.

WARREN W. WIERSBE

INTRODUCTION

ONE Sunday evening, about twenty years ago, I was standing in my pulpit at Hobart, Tasmania. The occasion was special and the church was crowded. I was commencing that night my Winter Series of Addresses. The addresses, as the printed syllabus showed, were to be delivered at fortnightly intervals. During the hymn before the announcements, I was deliberating on the precise phraseology in which I should refer to the course on which I was embarking. It suddenly flashed upon me that, by emphasizing the address that was to be delivered a fortnight hence, I was virtually inviting the more casual members of my congregation to absent themselves on the following Sunday. Could I not say a word that would make the intervening Sunday attractive? It happened that, during the week, I had been reading the Life of Luther, and had been impressed by the way in which the Reformation sprang from a single text.

Whilst I was still engrossed in this brown study, the hymn came to an end and the people resumed their seats. I announced my fortnightly addresses according to the printed syllabus; and then astonished myself by intimating that, on the following Sunday evening, I should commence an alternating series of fortnightly addresses entitled *The Texts That Made History*. 'Next Sunday evening,' I added, with extraordinary temerity, 'I shall deal with *Martin Luther's Text*!'

At the close of the service, one of my most trusted officers came to me in great delight. 'That's a noble idea,' he explained enthusiastically; 'it will be the best series that you ever preached!'

It has certainly been the longest, and the most evangelistic, and the most effective. And it has been the series in which I myself have found the most delight.

In taking leave of this fifth—and final—volume of the *Texts That Made History* Series, I felt that I should like to append this word of explanation.

FRANK W. BOREHAM

ARMADALE, MELBOURNE, AUSTRALIA

1

WILLIAM LAW'S TEXT

1686–1761

Writer who greatly influenced the English Evangelical Revival.

1 John 4:19

I

ALTHOUGH they appear to be thoroughly enjoying their mutton chop in the hospitable old dining-room of the Bull Inn at Putney, anybody can see at a glance that these two men are by no means at home in each other's society. They are, indeed, an ill-assorted pair. The one is a grave old clergyman; the other—a young fellow of twenty-two—is an obvious dandy. The one is the essence of simplicity; the other is the essence of affectation. Yet both are worth closer scrutiny, for the old gentleman has written a book that has stirred the sluggish conscience of the eighteenth century to its very depths; whilst his companion, in spite of the gay kerchief that he so ostentatiously flutters and the golden snuff-box that he so frequently taps, is destined to become the greatest historian of all time. For the old clergyman is William Law and the foppish young fellow who shares his table is Edward Gibbon.

Mr. Law, a thick-set, heavily built man, rather above the middle height, is in his seventy-fourth year. Although he has all his life practised the habits of a student, and for many years cultivated the soul of an ascetic, he has the face of a farmer, jolly and round, with red cheeks and gray eyes of unusual brightness. His very appearance conveys a subtle impression of immense strength and unfailing kindliness.

Gibbon, on the other hand, is a slight figure, dressed in a suit of flowered velvet. He is a nervous little creature of quickly moving hands and restless eyes, of fair hair faultlessly arranged and daintily powdered, of depressed nose and large, protuberant cheeks. It is hard on one who is so eager to cut a handsome figure in society that nature has done so little to promote this end.

By what strange freak of circumstance do these two men, having so little in common, happen to be dining together amidst the softness of this autumn sunshine in 1759? They are not strangers. In 1720, or thereabouts, Gibbon's grandfather engaged Mr. Law—then a young man of thirty-four—as a private tutor to his son, the father of the future historian. In that charming home at Putney the young minister quickly won his way into the affection of the entire household. He was treated as a member of the family. There he spent some of the happiest years of his life; there he received his guests as freely as if the stately residence had been actually his own; and there he wrote the book that has made his name immortal. At about the time of Gibbon's birth his grandfather died, and the home was broken up. But,

to the very end of Mr. Law's long life, all the members of the Gibbon family kept in closest touch with
him, holding him in highest honor and deepest
reverence.   Gibbon   himself   was   no   exception.
Although by temperament and training he was un-
fitted to appreciate the choicest qualities in the
character of the old man, he made no secret of
the profound respect and admiration in which he held
him.   He could not understand Mr. Law's religious
views—regarded them, indeed, as arrant nonsense—
yet, as long as he lived, he spoke with deep emotion
of his unwavering integrity and downright goodness
of heart.   'In our family,' Gibbon tells us in his
Memoirs, 'in our family William Law left the reputation of a worthy and pious man who believed all that
he professed, and practised all that he enjoined.' And
he was often heard to say that the beautiful character
of William Law had done more to make Christianity
credible to him than all the volumes of polemics
and apologetics over which it had been his duty
to pore.

So here they are, this apparently incongruous and
ill-matched pair, the one in sombre broadcloth and
the other in patterned velvet.   They stand in striking
contrast to each other; there seem to be no standards
by which we can compare them.   And yet, in his
Res Judicatae, the Right Hon. Augustine Birrell has
essayed that difficult task.   He speaks of Gibbon's
Decline and Fall of the Roman Empire as a most

splendid achievement of learning and industry; a glorious monument, more lasting than marble, to the unrivalled genius of its author. Yet Mr. Birrell adds we find ourselves at times in a mood in which the *Decline and Fall of the Roman Empire* seems but a poor and barren thing by the side of William Law's *Serious Call*—a book which has proven its power to pierce the hardest heart and tame the most stubborn will.

Gibbon has just returned from his long exile at Lausanne. He has been four years on the Continent under the tuition of Mr. Pavilliard. But now, to his unbounded delight, he is back in England; and the very fact that, after so protracted an absence, he is largely a stranger in his native land, makes him eager to renew, as quickly as possible, old ties and friendships. That is why, in the misty sunshine of this bright autumn day, these two are dining amidst scenes with which both are wonderfully and fondly familiar.

Before rising from the table, they sit chatting for a while. The younger man has much to say concerning his experiences abroad; the elder, dropping into reminiscence, talks of old times in this very neighborhood. Unconsciously they bend toward each other, with arms resting on the table. Thus situated, the quick and restless eye of Gibbon is arrested by the signet ring on the old man's hand. It bears an inscription, and, his curiosity awakened, he craves permission to examine it.

'I fear that the words are nearly worn off,' replies the gentle old man with a smile, 'but, originally, the inscription consisted of two Greek words: *Agapomen: Egapesen.*'

'*Love . . . loved,*' suggests the puzzled student, attempting to interpret the phrases.

'You will never make them out,' answers the other, smiling again; 'they are the two keywords in a passage from the New Testament, a passage that, through all my life, has meant very much to me—WE LOVE HIM BECAUSE HE FIRST LOVED US.'

The explanation has lifted the conversation to a plane out of the young man's reach. He does not wish to pursue it. Pushing back his chair with a casual question as to the direction that their afternoon stroll shall take, he prepares to leave the inn. And, a minute or two later, they vanish around the bend of the road. So far as our present study is concerned, we shall see no more of the gay kerchief, the gold snuff-box, and the velvet suit. For Mr. Law we must find another companion.

II

And we shall have no difficulty. For, very shortly after the happy household at Putney had been disbanded, and whilst Edward Gibbon was yet in his cradle, Mr. Law received a letter that stung him to

the quick. He had just settled down to his new life
at King's Cliffe. At five o'clock every morning he
entered his study, and, from that hour until late at
night, he made it his supreme endeavor to translate
into actual experience the lofty ideal that he had set
before the world in his *Serious Call*. Dr. Alexander
Whyte declares that, in the whole range of Christian
biography, there is nothing more arresting, more
impressive, or more instructive than the story of
Law's life of study, devotion, and charity during
those twenty years in the old mansion-house at
King's Cliffe.

But one morning he received a letter. It was from
John Wesley—not from the mature and mellow
Wesley, the Wesley of the silver locks, the Wesley
that we all love, but from a younger and harsher
Wesley; a Wesley who was self-opinionated and dic-
tatorial; a Wesley whose soul had not yet been
sweetened by the fullness of redeeming grace. When
he wrote that letter, Wesley was thirty-five; Law
was fifty-two. And the letter itself?

Now, sir [it reads], how will you answer to our common
Lord that you, sir, never led me into light? Why did I
scarcely ever hear you name *the name of Christ?* Why did
you never urge me to *faith in His blood?* Is not Christ the
First and the Last? If you say that you thought I had
faith already, verily, you know nothing of me. I beseech
you, sir, by the mercies of God, to consider whether the true
reason of your never pressing this salvation upon me was
not this—*that you never had it yourself!*

Many a time, in the years that followed, Wesley regretted, and regretted bitterly, the writing of that letter. But we must make allowance for him. For the history of Wesley, like the history of the world, divides itself into two parts—the B. C. part and the A. D. part. There is the part, that is to say, that precedes the memorable experience at Aldersgate Street on May 24, 1738, and there is the part that follows it. The letter was written ten days before that transforming and transfiguring event took place. Poor Wesley was in the depths of despair. He was enshrouded in that dense darkness that comes just before the dawn. He was like a hunted creature that in a desperate situation sees an avenue of escape from its pursuers, but cannot find a way into it. In his deep misery he was inclined to blame everybody who had played any part in directing his past pilgrimage.

In writing that angry letter, Wesley forgot four things.

(1) He forgot a certain occasion—two or three years earlier—on which he and his brother Charles had trudged sixty weary miles that they might confer with Mr. Law as to their spiritual perplexities, 'for,' as John afterwards confessed, 'Mr. Law was an oracle unto me in those days.' Mr. Law received the two brothers with great cordiality, and listened patiently and sympathetically to their story. And this was his reply:

You are groping [he said] after a purely philosophical religion.   There can be no such thing.   Religion is the plainest and simplest thing in the world.   It is just this: WE LOVE HIM BECAUSE HE FIRST LOVED US.

Much later in life Mr. Wesley—the Wesley of the silver locks—said that he never forgot that remark; but it must have slipped his mind on the day on which he wrote his terrible letter.

(2) He forgot, too, that he owed it to Mr. Law that he had been brought within sight of the Kingdom.   He read the *Serious Call* soon after it was published, and it affected him as it had affected so many others.   'I found Law,' Dr. Johnson admits, 'quite an overmatch for me.   And this was the first occasion of my thinking in earnest of religion after I became capable of religious inquiry.'

'Froude,' said John Keble one day, 'you told me that Law's *Serious Call* was a clever book.   I read it; and it seems to me now as if you had said that the Day of Judgement will be a pretty sight!'

It is a noble book, a wonderful book, a terrible book!   It cuts to the quick, as Dr. Whyte had said. As young Wesley turned its pages it convinced him, he tells us, of the absolute impossibility of being half a Christian.

I saw as I had never seen before [he says] the exceeding height, and depth, and length, and breadth of the law of God. The light flowed in so mightily upon my soul, that everything appeared in a new view and I cried unto God for help.

The *Serious Call* may not have led Wesley into the fullness of the light; but it certainly helped him on the way and quickened his steps towards his goal.

(3) He forgot that, since writing the *Serious Call*, and since the days in which, as an undergraduate, he himself had trudged long miles to consult his oracle, Mr. Law had passed through a profound and notable experience. For, just as there are two Wesleys, so there are two Laws. The first Wesley is separated from the second Wesley by the new light that broke upon him at Aldersgate Street on May 24, 1738. The first Law is separated from the second Law by the new light that broke upon him when he met with Jacob Behmen. Before Wesley went to the meeting at Aldersgate Street, he had been to America as a missionary to the Red Indians; but he could not convert them, he said, because he was not himself converted. Before Law met Jacob Behmen he had written the *Serious Call;* but he recognized, as soon as the new illumination came to him, that the gospel of the *Serious Call* was a crepuscular gospel, the gospel of the twilight, and he resolves henceforth to preach the gospel of high noon. 'It is difficult,' as Mr. Overton confesses in his *Life of William Law,* 'it is difficult to conceive of anyone permanently resting content with the system of the *Serious Call.*' Dr. Johnson could not; John Wesley could not; William Law' himself could not. And so, a year or two before he quitted the home of the Gibbons at

Putney, and two or three years before the illustrious historian was born, William Law entered into a spiritual affluence immensely greater than any thing that he had previously known. 'When I first began to read Behmen's book,' he tells us, 'it put me into a perfect sweat; but I digged and digged until I discovered the wonderful treasure hid in the field.'

We can scarcely blame Wesley for ignoring, in a letter written ten days before the great change came to him, the spiritual development of which his old oracle had been the subject; but afterwards, as he contrasted the Wesley that followed 1738 with the Wesley that preceded it, he cherished a kindlier feeling for the Law of the pre-Behmen days.

(4) He forgot, too, that no two men, however admirable, see the same object from precisely the same standpoint. Each of us has a distinct and individual view of every feature on the landscape. Nobody else sees it exactly as we do. To the end of his days, John Wesley never quite understood William Law. He was afraid that Jacob Behmen had carried his old teacher too far. Behmen made Law a mystic. Dean Inge says that the works of Law, after he came under the influence of Behmen, are among the finest mystical literature in our language. It was a mysticism that had iron in its blood—a practical mysticism. William Law gave all that he possessed to the poor. He received on one occasion an anonymous gift of a thousand pounds. He at once hurried off and en-

dowed an orphanage with the money. But Mr.
Wesley, jealous of the spiritual welfare of his early
instructor, was very suspicious of this mystical
development. At about the time at which we saw
Law and Gibbon dining at the Bull Inn, Law being
then on the brink of the grave, Mr. Wesley writes
him another letter. It is a kindlier letter than the
first, for Wesley is fast becoming the Wesley of the
silver locks, but still it is a protest and a plea. He
earnestly implored Mr. Law to eschew all mysticism.

'Come back,' he says, with an obvious reference to
that memorable interview of his student days, 'come
back to the plain religion of the Bible: WE LOVE
HIM BECAUSE HE FIRST LOVED US.'

We may smile at the argumentative epistles that
Wesley addressed to Law, and may even find the con-
troversy tedious. But there is something extremely
beautiful in the concern of Wesley lest his old master
should drift into a faith that is something less than
the very best.

III

But he need not have worried. For if, before he
met Behmen, Law was convinced that his text—WE
LOVE HIM BECAUSE HE FIRST LOVED US
—was the very heart and substance of the gospel, he
became still more emphatic on that point in the years
that followed. All his later books are concerned

almost exclusively with the amazing **love of God.**
'His theological system,' as Bishop Ewing points out,
'rests upon one only basis—that God is love—love
from eternity to eternity—and infinite, fathomless
depth of never-ceasing love.' And he himself
records his unalterable determination to proclaim un-
ceasingly the love of God—the love that gave its all;
the love that suffered on the bitter cross; the love
that regenerates the soul from above; the love that
blots out all transgressions; the love that robs temp-
tation of its powers and death of its sting.

In that serene confidence—a perfect confidence in
the everlasting love—he passed away. His death-
bed, it is said, was one long rapture. It was at
Eastertime, not many months after that dinner
with Gibbon at Putney. His last outing was to the
service on Easter Sunday morning. On his way
home, charmed by the beauties of the English spring-
time, he opened a gate, and, taking his companion's
arm, led him into the fields. And there, encompassed
by the fragrance of flowers, the hum of insects, and
the song of birds, he spoke with ecstasy of the
raptures of the life to come. As he lay dying a day
or two later, he talked of nothing but love—the love
of Christ and the love that, in his own heart, that
divine affection had begotten. *We love Him because
He first loved us.*

Those who seek the quiet and peaceful spot in
which he was laid to rest will have no difficulty in

finding it, for it is marked by the monument which Miss Gibbon, the aunt of the historian, erected to his honored memory. It was exquisitely fitting, as his biographer has said, that the body of such a man should be committed to the grave whilst the old church near by was still ringing with the echoes of the Easter music, and whilst Nature all around was unfolding, in every opening flower and budding hedgerow, her graceful and eloquent parable of the resurrection.

2

ABRAHAM LINCOLN'S TEXT

1809–1865

Sixteenth president of the United States.

Exodus 20:1–17

I

THE massive personality of Abraham Lincoln is like a granite boulder torn from a rugged hill-side. Too gigantic to be localized, he bursts all the bounds of nationality and takes his place in history as a huge cosmopolite. He belongs, as Edwin Stanton so finely exclaimed, in announcing that the last breath of the assassinated President had been drawn, he belongs henceforth to the ages! With the fine stroke and gesture of a king, he piloted the civilization of the West through the most momentous crisis of its history; and, in doing so, he established principles which will stand as the landmarks of statecraft as long as the world endures.

He was an immense human. As Edwin Markham sings:

> The color of the ground was in him, the red earth;
> The smack and tang of elemental things;
> The rectitude and patience of the cliff;
> The goodwill of the rain that loves all leaves;
> The friendly welcome of the wayside well;
> The courage of the bird that dares the sea;
> The gladness of the wind that shakes the corn;
> The pity of the snow that hides all scars.

Some men are far mightier than their achieve-
ments. What they *do* is great; but what they *are* is
infinitely greater. Abraham Lincoln is the outstanding example of the men of this towering and
gigantic cast. The world contains millions of people
who know little of American history, and who have
but the haziest notion as to the issues at stake in the
Civil War, yet upon whose ears the name of
Abraham Lincoln falls like an encrusted tradition,
like a golden legend, like a brave, inspiring song.

For one thing, we all seem to have seen him. We
are extraordinarily familiar with his long, lean,
sallow face; his leathery cheeks; his large, protruding
ears; his dreamy, melancholy eyes, his tumbled, wayward hair; his six-feet-four of bony awkwardness.
At the mere mention of his name, that gawky,
angular, and ill-proportioned form—long arms, long
legs, enormous hands and feet—garbed in the clothes
that never seem to fit, shambles its uncouth way before our eyes. His coats were the despair of his
tailor, and his battered hats nearly broke the heart
of his wife. In more ways than one, Lincoln was
terribly handicapped. In temperament, as well as
in appearance, he had much to overcome. At the out-
set of his career he was not only unattractive and
illiterate, he was self-opinionated, overbearing, and
abominably ill-mannered. Women, especially, were
repelled by him. One lady told him frankly that he
was never ready with those little gracious acts and

attentions which ladies so highly and so rightly
value, though, in the next breath, she admitted that
he had a heart full of kindness and a head full of
common sense. The anecdotes that lent piquancy
to his earlier speeches were too coarse to be printed.
In a word, he was, in those days, scarcely a gentleman. It is only against this background that we can
properly appreciate his triumph. He developed an
infinite capacity for self-culture. Awaking to the
fact that he was boorish, clumsy, and unpleasing, he
set himself steadfastly to work to remedy these
formidable defects. To this severe task he applied
himself so successfully that he became, in the end,
one of the most finished orators of his time, one of
the most powerful statesmen that the world has ever
seen, and one of the most perfect gentlemen that any
society could desire.

And, beyond the shadow of a doubt, it was by
means of his faith that he did it. His faith, it has
been said, was not of the orthodox type. Nor were
his features. But his faith, like his features, suited
him. In a famous ode, Lowell sings of the sublime
simplicity of Lincoln's faith; it produced, he says,
'the brave old wisdom of sincerity.' Emerson holds
that the majestic simplicity of Lincoln's faith is the
subtle secret that alone explains the splendor of his
eloquence. Tolstoy describes him as 'a miniature
Christ,' whilst Father Chiniquy, a Roman Catholic,
found in him the most perfect type of Christian.

In view of all this, an analysis of the rise and progress of Lincoln's faith is particularly alluring. It divides itself into three distinct phases. There is the *Iron Age* of his faith; there is the *Age of Clay;* and there is the *Golden Age.* Each is worth a glance.

II

Lincoln climbed Mount Sinai with Moses: that was how the *Iron Age* began. He was born in the midst of that tumultuous religious upheaval—that backwoods revival—which stands inseparably connected with the name of Peter Cartwright. He was, in a peculiar sense, the child of the camp-meeting. A tradition, cited by Judge Herndon, declares that, a few years before his birth, a certain camp-meeting had been in progress for several days. Religious fervor ran at fever heat. Gathered in complete accord, the company awaited with awed intensity the falling of the celestial fire. Suddenly the camp was stirred. Something extraordinary had happened. The kneeling multitude sprang to its feet and broke into a chorus of shouts which rang through the primeval shades.

A young man, who had been absorbed in prayer, began leaping, dancing, and shouting. Simultaneously, a young woman sprang forward, her hat falling to the ground, her hair tumbling about her shoulders in graceful braids, her eyes fixed heaven-

wards her lips vocal with strange, unearthly song.
Her rapture increased until, grasping the hand of the
young man, they blended their voices in ecstatic
melody. These two, the records assures us, were
married a week later and became the parents of
Abraham Lincoln.

By the time that the boy had reached years of
intelligent observation, however, this strange movement had changed its character. It became ethical
rather than emotional. Even Peter Cartwright
devoted himself to rebuking the political corruptions
and commercial depravities that were eating into the
heart of society. The red-hot propaganda of an
earlier day crystallized into a passionate insistence
upon national and individual righteousness.

Abraham Lincoln's young mother died when he
was barely nine. Her husband had to nurse her,
close her eyes, make her coffin, and dig her grave.
Abraham helped him carry that melancholy burden
from the desolated cabin to its lonely resting-place in
the woods. He never forgot that mother of his.
'All that I am,' he used to say, 'my angel-mother
made me!' And the memory that lingered longest
was the thought of her as she sat in the old log-cabin
teaching him the *Ten Commandments*. Many a time
afterwards, when he was asked how he had found
the courage to decline some tempting bribe, or to
resist some particularly insidious suggestion, he said
that, in the critical hour, he heard his mother's voice

repeating once more the old, old words: *I am the Lord thy God; thou shalt have no other gods before Me.* He treasured all through life her last words:

> I am going away from you, Abraham, and shall not return [she said]. I know that you will be a good boy, and that you will be kind to your father. I want you to live as I have taught you, to love your Heavenly Father and keep His commandments.

'*Keep His commandments!*' It was thus that, in infancy, Abraham Lincoln climbed Mount Sinai. It was thus that the Iron Age of his religious history was inaugurated. As a result somebody said of him that he was the most honest lawyer west of China. 'He was quite indifferent to money,' as Mr. A. C. Benson points out; 'he defended poor clients for nothing, and would even remind opposing counsel of points against his own case which they had over-looked.' This phase of his spiritual pilgrimage was *augmented;* it was never *obliterated.* Christ comes into the soul not to destroy, but to fulfil, the law. Lincoln's earliest religious impressions imparted to his character a severity that contributed materially to its grandeur.

III

Lincoln climbed Mount Carmel with Elijah; that was how the *Age of Clay*—the plastic age—began. Elijah learned on Mount Carmel that his loneliness in the midst of unscrupulous foes mattered little so long as the God who Answereth by Fire was with him. Lincoln learned identically the same lesson when, in 1860, he left his old home at Springfield and turned his face toward Washington. It was for him the hour of destiny. President McKinley told us how, in that fateful hour, Lincoln received a flag from one of his admirers. On its silken folds he read, beautifully worked, the words:

'Be strong and of good courage; be not afraid, neither be thou dismayed: for the Lord thy God is with thee whithersoever thou goest. There shall not any man be able to stand before thee all the days of thy life. As I was with Moses, so shall I be with thee.'

The words inscribed on the flag became the keynote of this *second* phase of his experience. He was going to Washington to assume the Presidency. He felt—and said—that he was as much and as truly called to lead the American people as Moses was called to lead the Hebrew people. He regarded himself as a Man with a Mission. Indeed, he had *two* missions—one immediate and one remote. The *immediate* mission was the preservation of the Union; the *remote* mission was the abolition of slavery. On both issues he was in deadly earnest; for either cause he was prepared to die. And he knew perfectly well that death was not improbable. Plots were laid to assassinate him before he could reach Washington. But he never wavered; the words on the flag were constantly in his mind. At every wayside station crowds gathered to greet him. And Dr. Hill points out that, in addressing each of these groups, he declared emphatically that he was going forth in the name of the Living God. 'Not even Moses praying in the wilderness: *"If Thy presence go not with me, carry me not up hence,"* seemed more dependent on the divine air than did Lincoln as he slowly journeyed to Washington.'

In accepting the Presidency, Lincoln was very sure of God. It meant two things to him. It meant that he would be protected, sustained, directed, and prospered in his lofty enterprise; he was immortal until his work was done. But it meant more. He was intensely, almost painfully, conscious of his own disqualifications and disabilities. He was a backwoodsman on his way to the White House! But he believed that—according to the promise on the flag— God was with him. Like Moses, he would be clay in the hands of the divine Potter; and, by those Unseen Hands, he would be moulded and shaped and fashioned. Here lies the secret of that ceaseless development and complete transformation which, as Lord Charnwood says, is the most amazing thing about him. It is for this reason that I have called this second phase the *Age of Clay*. It is the plastic, pliable, formative period of Lincoln's inner life. Yet it is by no means the climax.

IV

Lincoln climbed Mount Calvary with John: that
was how the *Golden Age* began.   But before Calvary
comes Gethsemane; and certainly Lincoln passed
through that Garden of Anguish.   Mr. H. C.
Whitney says that, during the war, Lincoln's companions would leave him by the fireside at night and
find him still there—elbows on knees and face in
hands—when they came down in the morning.
'Father,' he would moan again and again, *'Father, if
it be possible, let this cup pass from me!'*   Late one
Sunday night he called on Henry Ward Beecher,
looking 'so bowed with care, so broken by the
sorrows of the nation,' that it was difficult even to
recognize him.   A look of unutterable weariness had
crept into his sunken eyes.   'I think,' he confided to
a friend, 'I think I shall never be glad again.'   Yet,
as Dr. Hill points out, it was this discipline of suffering that rendered his faith irresistible and
triumphant.   But how?   The greatest grief of his
life was the death of his son.   As the boy lay dying,
Lincoln's reason seemed in peril.   Miss Ida Tarbell
has told the sad story with great delicacy and judgement.   When the dread blow fell, the nurse and the
father stood with bowed heads beside the dead boy,
and then the nurse, out of her own deep experience
of human sorrow and of divine comfort, pointed
the weeping President to her Saviour.

The work that this *private* sorrow began the *public* sorrow completed. Lincoln had long yearned for a fuller, sweeter, more satisfying faith. 'I have been reading the Beatitudes,' he tells a friend, 'and can at least claim the blessing that is pronounced upon those who *hunger and thirst after righteousness.*' He was to hunger no longer. A few days before his death he told of the way in which the peace of heaven stole into his heart. 'When I left Springfield,' he said, not without a thought of the flag and its inscription, 'when I left Springfield, I asked the people to pray for me; I was not a Christian. When I buried my son—the severest trial of my life—I was not a Christian. But when I went to Gettysburg, and saw the graves of thousands of our soldiers, I then and there consecrated myself to Christ.' From that moment, Dr. Hill says, the habitual attitude of his mind was expressed in the words: *'God be merciful to me, a sinner!'* With tears in his eyes he told his friends that he had at last found the faith that he had longed for. He realized, he said, that his heart was changed, and that he loved the Saviour. The President was at the Cross!

V

Happily, he lived to see the sunshine that followed the storm. He lived to see Peace and Union and Emancipation triumphant. His last hours were spent amidst services of thanksgiving and festivals of rejoicing. One of these celebrations was being held in Ford's Theatre at Washington. The President was there, and attracted as much attention as the actors. But his mind was not on the play. Indeed, it was nearly over when he arrived. He leaned forward, talking, under his breath, to Mrs. Lincoln. Now that the war was over, he said, he would like to take her for a tour of the East. They would visit Palestine—would see Gethsemane and Calvary—would walk together the streets of Jeru——!

But before the word was finished, a pistol-shot—the 'maddest pistol-shot in the history of the ages'—rang through the theatre. And he who had climbed Mount Sinai with Moses, Mount Carmel with Elijah, and Mount Calvary with John, had turned his pilgrim feet towards the holiest heights of all.

3

JO THE CROSSING-SWEEPER'S TEXT

Outlaw and waif in Charles Dicken's *Bleak House.*

Matthew 6:9–13

I

POOR Jo was being moved on for the last time. He was moving on, as he himself said, 'as fur as ever he could move.' Jo, as every reader of *Bleak House* well knows, was just a crossing-sweeper—the outlaw with the broom, as Dickens calls him. He was a mere waif, a city arab, part of the flotsam and jetsam of the life of London. Ask him his surname—he doesn't know! His age—he doesn't know!

'What's gone of your father and mother?' inquired Guster.

'I neber know'd nothink about 'em!' Jo replies.

That, as Dickens says, sums up his mental condition. He 'don't know nothink' about anything. He only knows that it is hard to keep the mud off the crossing in dirty weather, and harder still to live by doing it. Nobody taught him even that much; he found it out for himself. One other thing Jo has discovered. He has found out that there is no place for him in the world. He is incessantly being moved on.

'I'm always a-moving on, sir!' Jo once retorted in desperation, wiping away his grimy tears with his grimy arm. 'I've always been a-moving on and a-moving on ever since I was born. Where can I possibly move to more nor I do move?'

'My instructions don't go to that,' answered the constable. 'My instructions are that you are to move on; I've told you five hundred times!'

Perhaps more; the occasions were never counted. But now Jo is being moved on for the last time. He is being moved on by that grim, cold, relentless hand which sooner or later moves us all on.

'I'm being froze,' he cries, in the delirium of his fever, 'I'm being froze and then burnt up, and then froze and then burnt up, ever so many times in an hour. I'm being moved on and moved on more nor ever I was before. Every one of 'em's doing it, from the time when I don't get up to the time when I don't go to bed. I'm a-going somewheres; that's where I'm a-going!'

Dr. Allan Woodcourt is with him at the end. Jo lies dying in the back room of a shooting-gallery.

'It's turnin' wery dark, sir,' he exclaims; 'is there any light a-comin'?'

'It is coming fast, Jo,' replies the doctor. 'Jo, my poor fellow, do you hear me?'

'I hear you, sir, in the dark; but I'm a-gropin'— a-gropin'. Let me catch hold of your hand.'

'Jo, can you say what I say?'

'I'll say anythink as you say, sir, for I know it's good.'

' "*Our Father*" '

' "*Our Father*"—yes, that's *wery* good, sir.'

' "*Which art in heaven.*" '

' "*Art in heaven.*" Is the light a-comin', sir?'

'It is close at hand. *"Hallowed be Thy Name.'* ".

' "*Hallowed be Thy* . . . " '

The light had come. Jo had moved on. He who 'never know'd nothink' about father or mother had entered into a real sense of sonship at last.

' "*Our Father*"—that's wery good sir!' It is indeed.

II

The pity of it is that the Lord's Prayer is one of those sublime passages that have come to sound like platitudes through constant repetition. If only we could hear its majestic cadences with Jo's ears! If only we could re-discover their grandeur and pathos! We should feel a strange warmth stealing into our hearts and a strange moisture into our eyes. We should find ourselves saying with poor Jo: 'That's wery good, sir; wery good!'

The biographers of Edwin Booth, the distinguished American actor, bear eloquent witness to the eminent tragedian's profound affection for the Scriptures. Although his professional duties necessitated his spending half his time with Shakespeare and the great masters, he loved to leave them all behind and to steal away to his Bible. From every point of

view, he used to say, it was absolutely incomparable.
Whenever, in some select circle of friends, he was
asked to recite, he invariably selected some noble
passage from Job or David or Isaiah. Those who
heard him on such occasions declare that it really
seemed as if the ancient prophet had risen from
the dead and was unfolding with startling energy
the divine vision that had been vouchsafed to him.
On one such occasion, an elderly gentleman, who
had often maintained that very few of those who
regularly use the Lord's Prayer have realized its
stateliness and splendor, asked Booth to recite it.
For a moment the actor hesitated. Then, slowly
and reverentially, he rose; and in a few minutes
every person in the drawing-room was overwhelmed
by two irresistible conceptions. Everybody was
awed by the immediate sense of the divine presence,
whilst each separate individual seemed transformed
into a poor, sinning, stumbling, benighted, needy
suppliant, offering homage, asking bread, craving
pardon, light, and guidance.

'It was wonderful,' says one who was present that
evening, 'it was wonderful to watch the play of
emotion that convulsed Mr. Booth's countenance.
He became deathly pale, his eyes wet with tears. As
yet he had not spoken. The silence could be felt; it
had become absolutely painful; until at last the spell
was broken as his rich-toned voice syllabled forth,
"Our Father, which art in heaven," with a pathos

and fervid solemnity that thrilled all hearts. He finished; the silence continued; not a voice was heard, not a muscle relaxed, in his rapt audience, until, from a remote corner of the room, a subdued sob was heard, and the old gentleman who had made the request stepped forward. With streaming eyes and tottering frame, he seized Mr. Booth by the hand.

' "Sir," he said, in broken accents, "you have afforded me a pleasure for which I shall for ever feel grateful. I am an old man, and every day, from boyhood to the present time, I thought I had repeated the Lord's Prayer; but I never heard it before —*never!*"

' "You are right," replied Booth; "to utter that prayer as it should be uttered caused me the severest study and labor for thirty years, and even now I am far from being satisfied with my success." '

III

It is a wonderful prayer, a masterpiece of spiritual architecture. It reaches from earth to heaven, and stretches away through the eternities. It seems to begin at a little child's bedside. Our Father—*Father!* —FATHER! It gradually climbs up until it achieves its climax in a blaze of that glory that no man can approach unto: *'For thine is the Kingdom, the power, and the glory.'* And then, like a river plunging into the ocean, it loses itself in the infinities: *'For ever and ever.'*

Within the compass of the Lord's Prayer one seems to meet with men of all kinds, classes, and conditions. I stand within the hush that its solemnity inspires, and, all at once, I hear the sound of many voices. I hear a *Child* talking to his Father, a *Worshipper* offering homage to some hallowed Name, a *Patriot* sighing for the expansion of a kingdom, an *Optimist* expressing his confidence that all the earth shall become subject to the heavenly will, a *Mendicant* craving bread, a *Penitent* imploring pardon, and a *Pilgrim* feeling himself to be on a perilous path, and crying for direction and deliverance.

For the beauty of it is that the Lord's Prayer is *Everybody's Prayer*. The Master Himself taught it to His disciples; it was *theirs*. In Tissot's exquisite painting, 'The Lord's Prayer,' we seem to have seen Him, with His fishermen grouped around Him, as He teaches them, sentence by sentence, the noble petitions. The prayer became *their* prayer, the prayer of warm-hearted Peter and of the beloved John; but it was not theirs alone. It is the prayer of the devout, but it is also the prayer of the depraved. It is the prayer of the man who deplores the rebellion of his own heart: *'Our Father, Thy will be done! Thy Kingdom come!'* It is the prayer of the man who realizes that his soul is defiled with an indelible stain: *'Forgive our trespasses!'* It is the prayer of the man who feels himself to be shuddering on the brink of a terrible abyss, the sinner who is afraid of becoming a bigger sinner still: '*Deliver us from evil!*' It fits us all. It may be lisped by the little child at his mother's knee; it may be groaned by the criminal in the condemned cell. Within the sanctuary of the Lord's Prayer there is a place for each of us, a place that we each feel to be peculiarly our own. For the Lord's Prayer is *Everybody's Prayer.*

That was the discovery which so surprised and delighted Thomas Carlyle. He is over seventy, tortured by insomnia. But, writing to his old friend Thomas Erskine of Linlathen, he tells of an experience that has greatly refreshed him:

The other night in my sleepless tossings about, which were growing more and more miserable, that brief and grand prayer came strangely into my mind with an altogether new emphasis, as if written up and shining for me against the black bosom of the night, where I read it word by word, '*Our Father, which art in heaven, Hallowed be Thy Name, Thy will be done.*' It brought a sudden check to my fevered wanderings, a sudden softness of composure which was completely unexpected. I had never felt before how intensely the voice of man's soul that prayer is; the inmost aspiration of all that is highest and best in poor human nature.

The voice of man's soul! The inmost aspiration of our nature! Carlyle is right. The first instinct of our *physical* nature is to reach out blind hands in search of an earthly mother; the first instinct of our *spiritual* nature is to reach out blind hands in search of a Heavenly Father: '*Our Father, which art in heaven.*'

IV

The simplest and most effective way of assessing the value of a thing that has become commonplace is to imagine ourselves suddenly deprived of it. Who can visualize the world without the Lord's Prayer—a world without any sense of Fatherly love, of divine kingship, of daily providence or pardoning grace?

Half a century ago the finer susceptibilities of our literary critics were rudely shocked by the publication of a volume bearing the terrible title, *Letters from Hell*. It turned out to be a translation of a Danish work, and bore on its title-page the imprimatur and recommendation of Dr. George Macdonald. It purports to be the correspondence of a lost soul. He tells us of his sufferings, of his deprivations, and of his thoughts about the present and the past. Everything looks strangely different as viewed from this new standpoint. He reflects on things that were.

'Was there not,' he asks, in the course of one of these painful reveries, 'was there not something, in the vanished time, that was called the Lord's Prayer, beginning: *"Our Father,"* a well of blessing to those who opened their hearts to it? Surely I seem to remember, but yet vainly I try to recall, the sacred words. They seem hovering about me as though I need but say *"Our Father,"* and all the rest must follow. I set out to say it but never get beyond *"Our Father."* I have sometimes repeated these two words ten, twenty, fifty times; but it is quite hopeless; they are empty, and meaningless. I just remember that there *is* a Father; but He is not *my* Father, and I am not His child. Yet I cannot refrain from racking my spirit for the once-blessed words. My soul is thirsting for their comfort; but I can find no drop of water to cool my tongue.'

No Fatherly love! Nothing sacred or hallowed! No divine sway! No perfect will to be done in hell as in heaven! No daily bounty! No tender assurance of pardon! No spirit of forgiveness—forgiving even as forgiven! No guiding hand! No deliverance from evil! No Kingdom; no power; no glory! It is the essence of desolation! Even Jo would have shuddered at the thought of it. Jo lived in a wretched, ruinous place known as Tom-all-alones. It was a black, evilsmelling, dilapidated street, its rags and filth breeding every kind of fever, and its damp and gloomy tenements infested by a hideous swarm of human misery. Yet, as Jo found to his delight, even the ragged citizens of Tom-all-alones were not shut out from the Fatherly love, the kindly providence, and the pardoning grace of the Lord's Prayer. . .'*That's wery good, sir!*' cried poor Jo as his faith laid hold on the priceless message, '*that's wery good!*'

'*I just remember,*' moans the remorse-stricken sufferer to whose words we have already listened, '*I just remember that there is a Father; but he is not my Father, and I am not His child!*'

V

It is a far cry from poor Jo's straw pallet in the shooting-gallery to the Red Indian encampments amidst the vast solitudes of the North American forests. But let us plume our wings for the flight; the journey, though a long one, will handsomely repay us.

For here, far back in the silent woods of Saskatchewan, three hundred chiefs and braves have assembled in solemn conclave. Early in the morning, in all the glory of feathers and moccasins, they form a circle, and, in the center of it there stands a white man—Mr. Egerton Young. To his fierce but picturesque congregation Mr. Young unfolds the story of the love of God. The seed falls on absolutely virgin soil; these men have heard nothing of the kind before.

When Mr. Young had finished, several of the chiefs questioned him. The last to speak, he tells us, was an old savage-looking man with long, grizzly hair and wild, excited movements.

'Missionary,' he explained, 'once my hair was as black as a crow's wing; now it is getting white. Grey hairs on my head and grandchildren in my wigwam tell me that I am getting old and have not long to live. Yet I have never heard such things as you have told us to-day. But, missionary, when you spoke just now to the Great Spirit, did I hear you say, "Our *Father*"?'

'Yes,' replies Mr. Young, " '*Our Father, which art in heaven.*' "

'That is very new and sweet to us,' continues the grizzled old chief, his eyes moistening; 'we never thought of the Great Spirit as *Father*. We heard Him in the thunder; we saw Him in the lightning, the tempest, and the blizzard; and we were afraid. So when you tell us that the Great Spirit is *our Father*, that is very beautiful to us! And, missionary, did you say that the Great Spirit is *your* Father?' . . .

'I did!'

'And is He *the Indian's* Father?'

'He is!'

'Then we are *brothers!*' the old man exclaims. And Mr. Young adds that, at this stage, the excitement of the whole company was a wonderful thing to see. With one accord they implored him to stay among them and expound his message more fully.

'*That is wery good!*' said poor Jo.

'*It is very new and sweet to us!*' cried the old Indian.

VI

But we shall probe to the quivering heart of the matter neither in the London shooting-gallery nor in the American forest. Let us go on a pilgrimage to Drumtochty, under the sure guidance of Ian

Maclaren. We have all shed a silent tear—a tear of
which we were unashamed—over *The Transformation of Lachlan Campbell.* It is a lovely story. The
transformation itself is a most wonderful thing. It
seems incredible that the stern old Lachlan Campbell,
who, at the beginning of the story, can strike his
prodigal daughter's name out of the family Bible,
can be one with the gentle old man who, at the end of
the story, covers himself with self-reproaches, re-
joices over Flora's return, and enfolds her in a love
that is as gentle as a mother's. And the climax of
the *Transformation* is reached when Flora and her
father once more kneel together in family worship.
For, that night, Ian Maclaren says, the old man began his prayer : *'Our Father!'* 'It was a new word for
Lachlan ; he always used to say *Jehovah!'*

It was about this transformation that the Saviour
spoke when He took a little child and set him in the
midst of His disciples. *'Except ye be transformed,'*
He said, *'and become as this little child, ye shall not
enter into the Kingdom of Heaven.'* That is precisely
what happened at Drumtochty : Lachlan Campbell
became a little child. *'Our Father!'* he cried. The
words sound 'wery good,' as Jo would say ; and those
who, like Jo, have made the prayer their own, will
speak with similar ecstasy of its sweetness.

4

FRANCIS THOMPSON'S TEXT
1859–1907
English poet and author of "The Hound of Heaven."

Luke 19:10

I

DAWN is breaking on the Thames Embankment, and the unhappy creatures whose poverty has compelled them to spend the night among its shelters and recesses are beginning to stir. A steady drizzle is falling. Our attention is arrested by a forlorn-looking waif, a young man in his twenties, his toes peeping through his boots, his clothes in tatters, and his long hair and straggling beard appearing desperately wild and dishevelled. He shuffles from the stone seat, shivers, coughs, pulls himself together, and faces grimly the prospects of another weary day. Life has gone hardly with this man of late. He attempted to earn a few pence by selling matches, but failed. Then he tried newspapers; but the street arabs, with their sharp eyes and nimble feet, beat him hollow at that game. He scraped together a shilling or two and established himself as a bootblack, but the police ruined his chances by everlastingly moving him on. During the past week a solitary sixpence has come his way, earned by holding a horse's head. And so he sleeps—or at least spends the nights—on the Embankment, and lives—or at least exists—on any morsel that he can pick up.

And yet, if you were to search him, you would find among his ragged pockets a copy of Aeschylus, the poems of William Blake, and a dirty scrap of paper on which some indecipherable lines have been pencilled. Those lines are his own. For this is Francis Thompson, one of the purest poets and one of the choicest souls that England ever produced. To read his poems—many of which were first conceived and drafted in the days of his raggedness and wretchedness—is, as Katherine Tynan says, like setting sail with Drake or Hawkins in search of new worlds and golden spoils. Mr. J. L. Garvin ranks him with Milton. 'He is,' Mr. Garvin declares, 'an Argonaut of literature, far travelled in the realms of gold. *The Hound of Heaven* is the most wonderful lyric in the language. It fingers all the stops of the spirit. We hear now a thrilling and dolorous note of doom; now the choiring of the spheres; and now the very pipes of Pan; but, under all, the still, sad music of humanity. It is the return of the nineteenth century to Thomas à Kempis.' Milton! à Kempis! Francis Thompson! Clearly there is a matter here for closer investigation! And the first question is: How does it come about that, like a miser clinging desperately to the last coins of his former hoard, this London waif carries Aeschylus and Blake in his grimy pockets?

II

One does not need the bewildering acumen of a Sherlock Holmes in order to reach the deduction that, although Francis Thompson has plunged into the abyss, he is not a creature of the abyss. He has invaded a realm of which he is not a citizen, a realm from which he is destined gloriously to emerge. He was the son of a hard-working doctor in Lancashire; and his parents, who were by no means wealthy, subjected themselves to a severe but secret discipline of self-denial in order that they might educate their boy for his father's profession. The programme broke down hopelessly. Francis, although possessed of many excellent and engaging qualities, lacked his father's patience and persistence. He loved poking about the Manchester libraries and art galleries; he gloried in a cricket match, and especially a Test Match, at Old Trafford; but for close application and systematic study he had no mind. He spent eight years at Owens College. Year by year he went up for his examinations, and nearly broke his father's heart with the monotonous formula: 'I have not passed!' The doctor was desperate. His scanty savings—the fruit of the most rigid frugality—had all been squandered. And for what?

Francis was summoned to a family conference. The meeting was a stormy one. He arrived, looking flushed and agitated. He gave the impression that he had been drinking. His father accused him of it.

Francis indignantly denied the charge and bounced
out of the room. The household was mistaken. The
trouble was, not alcohol, but opium. His mother,
just before she died, had presented him with De
Quincey's *Confessions of an Opium Eater*. He read
it; coveted the gorgeous dreams that De Quincey
describes; took to opium (to which Lancashire cot-
ton-spinners of that time were commonly addicted);
and suffered an immediate slackening of his mental
powers.

Hungering for the unknown, Francis made his
way to London, and, for three hideous years, drank
of the dregs of that great city. He herded with the
lowest of the low and the vilest of the vile; and,
although he himself never became immoral or de-
based, he endured horrors that cruelly affected his
health and that remained like an indelible smudge
upon his soul.

III

There was a flutter of curiosity and excitement in
the office of a certain London journal on a memorable
April day in 1888. The editor, Mr. Wilfrid Meynell,
was informed that Mr. Francis Thompson, the brilliant but elusive contributor from whom he had received several mysterious packages of manuscript,
was actually on the premises. The first of these packages had reached Mr. Meynell in February, 1887.
It was accompanied by a letter enclosing a stamped

envelope for reply. The writer apologized for the soiled condition of the manuscript. It was due, he explained, not to slovenliness, but to the strange places and circumstances under which it had been written. In point of fact, some of those sheets had been scribbled in bed; some had been laid perpendicularly against a wall and some pencilled by the light of a street-lamp; some had been dashed by candlelight in a dingy corner of a common lodging-house. 'Kindly address your rejection,' said the sender, in a postscript, 'to the Charing Cross Post Office.' Realizing that he had struck gold, Mr. Meynell wrote at once, but the note came back through the Dead Letter Office. At length he decided to publish the poems, hoping that their appearance would reopen communications. The ruse succeeded.

Mr. Thompson was announced. 'Show him up!' said Mr. Meynell. The door opened; a strange apparition presented itself; drew back; opened the door again; drew back a second time; and, at the third venture, shambled in! Mr. Meynell could scarcely believe his eyes. The figure before him was more ragged and unkempt than the average beggar, with no shirt beneath his coat, and bare feet in broken shoes. Mr. Meynell sat speechless with astonishment. But the essential thing is that when, after all this nervous struggling with the editor's door, Francis Thompson at last screwed up courage to creep in, he,

by that very act, left the abyss for ever. He was a
wreck physically and socially. But, to their everlasting honor, Mr. and Mrs. Meynell took him into
their beautiful home; surrounded him with refinement, affection, and the laughter of happy children;
and, from that day to the day of his death, Francis
Thompson was one of the most loved and honored
personalities in English life and letters.

IV

The Hound of Heaven is a chaste and exquisite
record of the spiritual pilgrimage of Francis
Thompson during the years that he spent as a citizen
of the gutter. For, looking back upon it, he feels
that it was not so much a *descent* as a *pursuit*. He
was being hunted—hunted by Love—the Love that
would not let him go. This Tremendous Lover, as
he calls Him, shadowed his steps night and day
like a detective on the track of his quarry.

> I fled Him, down the nights and down the days;
>   I fled Him, down the arches of the years;
> I fled Him, down the labyrinthine ways
>   Of my own mind; and in the mist of tears
> I hid from Him, and under running laughter.
>
>   Up vistaed hopes, I sped;
>   And shot, precipitated,
> Adown Titanic glooms of chasmèd fears,
> From those strong Feet that followed, followed after.

> But with unhurrying chase,
> And unperturbèd pace,
> Deliberate speed, majestic instancy,
> They beat—and a Voice beat
> More instant than the Feet—
> 'All things betray thee, who betrayest Me.'

Whether he sauntered along Edgware Road, or turned his face towards the East End, or threw himself down, sick at heart, on the inhospitable stonework of the Embankment, he could never throw off his divine Pursuer. And how did it all end? Let the last lines of the poem tell—

> Now of that long pursuit
> Comes on at hand the bruit;
> That Voice is round me like a bursting sea:
> 'Lo, all things fly thee, for thou fliest Me!
> Alack, thou knowest not
> How little worthy of any love thou art!
> Whom wilt thou find to love ignoble thee,
> Save Me, save only Me?
> All which I took from thee I did but take,
> Not for thy harms,
> But just that thou might'st seek it in My arms.'
> 'Ah, fondest, blindest, weakest,
> I am He whom thou seekest!
> Thou dravest love from thee, who dravest Me.'

During those dreadful years, London throbbed with God. And, ever afterwards, the great city seemed to Francis Thompson to be the New Jerusalem. The angels hovered around Oxford Circus; the seraphim sang their 'Holy, Holy, Holy'

above the Mansion House and the Bank; Ezekiel's
life-giving river flowed from underneath St.Paul's!
After Thompson's death a little poem was found in
his desk. In it he speaks of

> . . . Jacob's ladder
> Pitched between heaven and Charing Cross;

and of

> . . . Christ walking on the water,
> Not of Gennesareth, but Thames.

It was through the highways and by-ways of
London that the *Hound of Heaven* pursued him; and
the highways and by-ways of London became trans-
figured in his eyes in consequence.

V

Francis Thompson had solid ground for his sublime conviction. He had good reasons for believing
that, even in the depths of the abyss, he was neither
left nor forsaken.

(1) In one of his poems he offers the homage of
his heart to the memory of a woman—a woman of
the city which was a sinner—who, in the abyss, took
pity upon him. 'This girl,' says the biography, 'gave
out of her scant and pitiable opulence, consisting of
a room, warmth, food, and a cab thereto. When the
streets were no longer crowded with shameful possi-

bilities she would think of poor Francis Thompson, would take her beggar into her vehicle at the appointed place, and would cherish him with an affection maidenly and motherly. Two outcasts, they sat marvelling that there were joys for them to unbury and to share.'

(2) Even when the worst came to the worst, heaven drew very near to him, he tells us repeatedly, when he looked into the faces of little children. Here is a memory of the Embankment; a night beneath the open sky. After telling how he 'suffered the trampling hoof of every hour,' and 'endured the abashless inquisition of each star,' he describes the tardy coming of the dawn:

> Then there came past
> A child; like thee, a spring-flower; but a flower
> Fallen from the budded coronal of spring,
> And through the city streets blown withering.
> She passed—O brave, sad, lovingest, tender thing!—
> And of her own scant pittance did she give,
> That I might eat and live:
> Then fled, a swift and trackless fugitive.

And again, in *The Hound of Heaven,* he tells us that:

> I sought no more that after which I strayed
> In face of man or maid;
> But still within the little children's eyes
> Seems something, something that replies,
> *They* at least are for me, surely for me!
> I turned me to them very wistfully.

(3) And how could he ever forget Mr. McMaster, the shoemaker of Panton Street? One night, when poor Francis was numb with cold, sick with starvation, and giddy with the glare of the streets, a hand was suddenly laid on his shoulder.

'Is your soul saved?' a voice inquired.

'What right have you to ask me that question?' Francis angrily replied.

'Ah, well,' exclaimed the good churchman, 'if you won't let me save your soul, let me save your body!'

And he insisted on taking Francis to his home and providing him with food and clothes and the chance of earning money.

(4) And then, of course, there was a climax when he fell in with Wilfrid and Alice Meynell. Such things as these do not happen in a God-forsaken world. They fastened upon the sensitive mind of Francis Thompson the conviction that he was divinely watched, divinely followed, divinely coveted, and divinely loved. The *Hound of Heaven* was at his heels all the time.

VI

Mr. Meynell, the genial benefactor and proud friend of the poet, describes Thompson as a moth of a man. For twenty years after his emergence from the abyss, he lived a frail but fruitful life, revelling in his work and honor by the most honorable in the land. 'Seldom,' says Mr. Le Gallienne, 'has the world seen a poet more wildly abandoned to his rapture, more absorbed in the trance of his ecstasy. When the irresistible moment comes, he throws himself upon his mood as a glad swimmer gives himself to the waves, careless whither the strong tide carries him, knowing only the wild joy of the laughing waters and the rainbow spray. He shouts for very gladness in the welter of wonderful words, and he dives, swift and fearless, to fetch his deep-sea fancies.' Happily, his father lived to marvel at his triumph. But Francis could not hope to live long. At the age of forty-eight, caressing Mr. Meynell's hand to the last limits of consciousness, he quietly passed away. In his coffin were roses from the garden of George Meredith, and on his breast were the violets that Mrs. Meynell placed there. 'A true poet,' wrote George Meredith on the card attached to the roses, 'a true poet, one of the small band.'

And so, amidst the roses and the violets, we leave him—a moth of a man; but a moth of a man with the soul of a seraph.

VII

Professor W. L. Phelps on one side of the Atlantic, and Dr. J. A. Hutton on the other, agree in comparing *The Hound of Heaven* with the one hundred and thirty-ninth Psalm: *'Whither shall I go from Thy spirit? or whither shall I flee from Thy presence? If I ascend up into heaven, Thou art there; if I make my bed in hell, behold, Thou art there. If I take the wings of the morning, and dwell in the uttermost parts of the sea; even there shall Thy hand lead me, and Thy right hand shall hold me.* Dr. Hutton and Dr. Phelps have been my trusted guides so often that I tremble to quit their company. Yet this time, I confess, they leave me cold. For, in spite of them, I find myself associating Francis Thompson, not with the seers of the Old Testament, but with the saints of the New. For, after all, who was the Tremendous Lover who followed Thompson all the way, and at whose feet he threw himself in perfect trust and submission at the last? It was the Eternal Seeker—the Good Shepherd who, rejoicing, bears upon his *shoulders* the sheep that, sorrowing, He has always borne upon His *heart.* Francis Thompson aspired to be known as a great evangelical poet. 'Call me,' he explained, 'not the Poet of the return to Nature, but the Poet of the return to God!' And one of his biographers declares that hundreds of the readers of *The Hound of Heaven* date their drawing to the Feet of the Tremendous Lover to the day when the poem's appealing music first broke on their encircling gloom. In Christ, Thompson declares in one of his essays, in Christ is solved the supreme problem of life! And, with a thought of death, he says in one of his poems that the last long beam of the setting sun will lie steady on the Cross!

The Tremendous Lover! Christ! The Cross! In view of all this, I seem to see, inscribed above Thompson's immortal poem, these great words: *'FOR THE SON OF MAN IS COME TO SEEK AND TO SAVE THAT WHICH IS LOST.'* That, beyond the shadow of a doubt, is *Francis Thompson's Text.*

5

JOHN HOWARD'S TEXT
c. 1726–1790
English prison reformer.

Psalm 17:15

I

SOME of the finest masterpieces of the world's most eminent sculptors now adorn the stately aisles of St. Paul's; but the *first* statue to be admitted to that sacred edifice was the statue of John Howard. In that interesting circumstance there is something symbolic. For Howard was essentially a pioneer. He did a work peculiarly his own in a way peculiarly his own. As Burke observed in 1781, when Howard was in the full tide of his career, 'His plan is original; it is marked as much by genius as by humanity. He has embarked on a voyage of discovery, a circumnavigation of charity. Already the benefit of his labors is felt in every civilized country. I cannot name this gentleman,' Burke went on to say, 'without remarking that his labors have opened the eyes of mankind. He has visited all Europe—not to survey the sumptuousness of palaces or the stateliness of temples; not to inspect the remains of ancient grandeur or to gaze with curiosity and admiration on the triumphs of modern art—but to dive into the depths of dungeons; to plunge into the infection of hospitals; to survey the mansions of sorrow and pain; to take the dimensions of misery, depression, and contempt; to remember the forgotten, to attend to the neglected, to visit the forsaken, and to alleviate the distresses of all men in all countries.' No man, as Dean Milman averred, in commenting on that pioneer monument at St. Paul's, no man ever did as much as Howard to assuage the misery of the world.

II

Never was a great historic work undertaken with so little premeditation and design. On November 1, 1775, the whole world heard with horror that the capital of Portugal had been destroyed by earthquake. Goethe and Voltaire have both described the stunning effect of the frightful news. 'The event arrested universal attention,' Goethe tells us; 'all men felt insecure; the demon of terror had never so speedily and powerfully stirred the earth.' In the hour of her calamity, Lisbon looked to London for help. 'This bitter cry,' says Mr. Hepworth Dixon, 'found Howard—then a youth of twenty-nine—sitting by the corpse of his dead wife. He heard it and sprang to his feet.' But what could *he* do? He would go! He would visit the actual spot! He would administer relief with his own hands! But the unexpected happened. He booked his passage on the *Hanover*. But England and France were at war. The *Hanover* was captured by a French privateer; and Howard, with his fellow passengers, was unceremoniously thrown into prison. During the two days that they had spent on the privateer they had been denied both food and water; and, on being shut up in the dungeon—'a horrible hole, dark, damp, and filthy beyond description'—they were again kept for several hours in a state of starvation. At last a leg of mutton was flung into the cell—as flesh is thrown into the dens of wild beasts—for the ravenous creatures to tear at, fight for, and greedily devour. They slept on the stone floor. This bitter and degrading experience set Howard thinking. Was it possible, he wondered, that *all* prisoners were subjected to such horrors as he had himself suffered? He would make it his business to find out. And thus, unsought and unexpected, his life-work came to him.

III

The discoveries that he made in the course of those voyages of exploration must, in our time, appear utterly incredible. In most every prison he found the unfortunate inmates, of both sexes herded together in one vile chamber, often underground, with little or nothing in the shape of light, ventilation, or sanitation. In many cases this abominable dungeon was so constructed that the open sewer of the town ran through it. The odor of the place was so disgusting that, after leaving it, Mr. Howard could never enter a room, or the interior of a stage coach, until he had enjoyed a bath and an entire change of clothes. If these conveniences were not available, he had to walk or ride on horseback, until he could obtain them. The fevers and pestilences that broke out in these horrid holes were so frightful that they not only swept away the prisoners in hundreds, but spread to the officials, to the crowds in the courts, and even to the judges. On more than one occasion Howard found among the prisoners the bodies of those who had been dead for days. It was no uncommon thing for a prisoner to be devoured by rats.

These crying evils sprang from one fruitful source. The officials received no salaries; indeed, they paid as much as forty pounds a year for their positions. They reaped their recompense in the fees that they wrung from their victims. No unhappy wretch could escape continuous torture, or obtain the slightest semblance of comfort, except by paying the jailer. And the worst of it was that the innocent suffered with the guilty. 'For,' says Howard, 'the thing that moved me most was the sight of those who had been found Not Guilty—and even those against whom no charge could justly be laid—suffering the same penalties as the most hardened and depraved criminals. After being confined for months awaiting trial, these unfortunates, though publicly acquitted, were again dragged back to jail and locked up with the other

prisoners until they could pay the fees that they owed
to the governor, the clerk of assize, the jailer, the
turnkey, and the likes.' Debt, too, was as much a
crime as highway robbery.   At Cardiff, Howard
found that a man had just died, after rotting for ten
years in a loathsome cell, for owing a tradesman
seven pound.   The whole thing, as Green says in his
Short History of the English People, was a perfect
chaos of cruelty.

With a case so unanswerable, Howard quickly
caught the ear of the public.   He had scarcely made
his voice heard when a Bill was introduced into Parliament *'for the relief of prisoners, for the abolition
of fees to jailers, and for the more effectually se-
curing the health of prisoners during their confinement.'*   Mr. Howard was called to the Bar of the
House of Commons, and was told by the Speaker
that the House was very sensible of the humanity and
zeal which had led him to visit the jails and to com-
municate to the House the observations he had made.
And then, the reform movement being afoot in
England, Mr. Howard left for the Continent to
initiate the same salutary crusade in every land.   He
allowed no personal danger to turn him from his
purpose.   He made his way to the Bastille, to the
French galleys, to the prisons of the Inquisition in
Spain, and to the lazarettos of Turkey.   He went
everywhere.   And neither the threats of exalted
officials, nor the ravages of the pestilence, balked

or deterred him. With as high a courage as has ever been displayed upon a battle-field, he dauntlessly persisted in his pilgrimage of pity.

IV

It was in the course of one of these innumerable voyages of research that this indomitable explorer made the most sublime discovery of his adventurous life. Let us look at him!

He is a small man, stout but well made, of dark complexion and brisk, eager movement. He has a lively eye, a bold Roman nose, and a cheerful, expressive countenance. He wears a pepper-and-salt coat, a scarlet waistcoat, and a cocked hat. It is the month of February, 1770; he is in his forty-fourth year, and is visiting The Hague. In his *Journal* he makes the following reflections, which mark, as his biographer says, 'a new development of the religious elements in his character':

HAGUE, *Sunday evening, February* 11, 1770.—I would record the goodness of God to the unworthiest of His creatures. I have had for some days past an habitual serious frame, repenting for my sin and folly, applying to the blood of Jesus Christ, and solemnly surrendering myself to Him. Oh, the wonders of redeeming love! Some faint hope have I, even I, that, through the full atoning Sacrifice, I shall ere long be made the monument of the rich, free grace and mercy of God through the divine Redeemer.

Some faint hope! That hope was abundantly

realized. For, three months later, at Naples, I find him preparing and signing a solemn covenant. 'This document,' as Mr. Dixon says, 'is the most important, in relation to his mental history, which we possess.'

NAPLES, *May 27*, 1770.—Lord, I believe; help Thou mine unbelief! Here, on this sacred day, in the dust before the Eternal God, I cast my guilty and polluted soul on the sovereign mercy of the Redeemer. Oh, compassionate and divine Lord, save me from the dreadful guilt and power of sin, and accept my solemn, free, and unreserved surrender! Look upon me, a repenting, returning prodigal! Thus, O Lord God, am I humbly bold to covenant with Thee! Ratify and confirm it, and make me the everlasting monument of Thy mercy. Glory to God—Father, Son, and Holy Ghost—for ever and ever. Amen and Amen.

This solemn covenant he periodically reviewed, minutely examining his life in the light of it. And, at Moscow, on September 27, 1789—shortly before his death—he definitely and formally renewed it.

From that moment Christ was everything to him —everything! 'I have no hope,' he writes to a friend, 'in anything that I have said or done. In Him, the Lord Jesus Christ, I trust. In Him I have strong consolation.' In 1778 he is overtaken by serious illness. 'Every refuge but Christ is a refuge of lies,' he tells in his *Journal;* 'my soul, stay thou upon the Rock!' 'God in Christ is the Rock and Portion of my soul,' he writes to Dr. Stennett some years later. In 1786 a great fund was raised in England with a view to erecting a statue in his honor. When the news reached him he was deeply hurt; he sternly and imperatively forbade the completion of the project. 'When I die,' he wrote, 'let a plain slab of marble be placed over my grave, with this inscription: "JOHN HOWARD, died—; aged—. *My hope is in Christ."*'

With John Howard, Christ was *first* and Christ was *last,* and Christ was *everything between.*

V

When, in 1789, he was preparing to leave England on one of his 'voyages of exploration,' his mind became obsessed with the conviction that he was going to his death. He was sixty-three, and prematurely aged. He was about to visit many of the plague centres of Europe, and was not blind to the risk. He paid farewell visits to his old friends, made a final disposition of his affairs, and handed little gifts to all his servants and helpers. He took a last fond look at the familiar scenes around his home. 'His hair had grown grey and his step feeble. As he tottered past them, bent with sorrow and labor, the villagers gazed on the brave old man, and the tears sprang to many eyes as, with grateful thoughts of his past goodness, they reflected that they would never hear his kindly voice again.'

He gave explicit instructions, Dr. Stoughton

tells us, concerning the *text* on which his funeral sermon was to be preached. 'I would have it based,' he
said, 'on the last verse of the seventeenth Psalm: *"As
for me, I will behold Thy face in righteousness: I
shall be satisfied, when I awake, with Thy likeness."*
That text is the most appropriate to my feelings of
any that I know.' At the same time he laid a strong
embargo on any attempt to hold him up to the admiration of survivors.

John Howard's *Text* is the natural climax of John
Howard's *trust*. 'My hope is in Christ,' he wrote
again and again. 'Christ is *everything* to me!' What
more natural than that now, in view of death, he
should long actually to behold his Lord?

I shall behold Thy face!
I shall be satisfied with Thy likeness.

'If,' says Thomas Watson, in his brief but telling
exposition of the text, 'if there be so much delight in
God when we see Him only by faith, what will be the
joy of vision when we see Him face to face?' *'As for
me, I will behold Thy face in righteousness: I shall be
satisfied, when I awake, with Thy likeness.'*

I have sometimes wondered: was Ruth Graham
Robinson thinking of John Howard when she penned
her lines on 'God's Forgiveness'?

> How doth our God forgive?
> Casting from sight
> Behind Him our sins, which He hates. Ah, but we,
> The sinners, His face shall in righteousness see!

No words could more perfectly express the gratitude with which Mr. Howard looked *backward* upon his conversion and *forward* to his translation.

VI

The inevitable happened. In ministering to an infected patient in southern Russia, he contracted a malignant fever, and was gone. 'Suffer no pomp to be used at my burial,' he begged. 'Lay me quietly in the earth; place a sundial over my grave; and let me be forgotten!' It was not in human nature to take such instructions seriously. The whole world mourned its benefactor. 'The cry of grief which arose on the Dnieper was echoed from the Thames,' says Mr. Dixon, 'and there were moist eyes on the Tagus, the Neva, and the Dardanelles. His death was not merely a national, it was a European, event. Never had mortal man such funeral honors as were heaped upon him.' He had visited the most loathsome scenes in every land. He had made himself the friend of the felon. On behalf of the most despised outcasts, he had stood before Parliaments and confronted kings and emperors. He had done a noble work, and done it well. He was, as John Wesley affirmed, one of the greatest men of his time. He was the pioneer of a new age, the founder of a new epoch. Statues and memorials sprang up everywhere. His name shines with a deathless

lustre.   But what is that to him?   He has found the
rapture that he so eagerly coveted.   *'As for me,'* he
seems to say, *'I behold His face in righteousness: I
am satisfied, abundantly satisfied, with His likeness.'*

6

PAUL GASPARD'S TEXT

Character in *The Gaspards of Pine Croft* by Ralph Connor.

Matthew 18:21–22

I

'*Remember—70 x 7!*'

It was by far the greatest lesson that Paul Gaspard ever learned; it was by far the greatest that he ever taught. It is Ralph Connor who tells his story. Many a novel has been written to illumine a text; but Ralph Connor has the distinction of having written two novels to illustrate the same passage of Scripture.

'*Then came Peter, and said, Lord, how often shall my brother sin against me, and I forgive him? till seven times? Jesus said unto him, I say not unto thee, Until seven times; but, Until seventy times seven.*'

The words stand embedded like a glittering gem in *The Doctor of Crows' Nest*. It is a story of two brothers—Dick and Barney Boyle. Dick does Barney a cruel wrong, and Barney carries a fierce hatred in his heart in consequence. Then comes the crisis of the story—the Gethsemane scene, as Ralph Connor himself calls it. The brothers meet, and, after an intense inner struggle, Barney forgives. From that hour he becomes a new man. The telling chapters that unfold this part of the story are entitled : 'Until Seventy Times Seven,' 'To Whom He Forgave Most,' and 'The Heart's True Rest.' These titles speak for themselves, and, since they speak for themselves, I need say no more about *The Doctor of Crows' Nest*. I am concerned just now with *The Gaspards of Pine Croft*.

II

Paul Gaspard learned his lesson for the first time at his mother's knee. He was a delicate, highly sensitive, extremely imaginative boy, quivering with intellectual intensity and passionate emotion. Life, for him, held two great experiences. The *first* was when he lay on his back under the tall pine-trees of the Windermere Valley and, watching the white clouds scudding across the blue, blue sky, convinced himself that he could see God looking earnestly down at him. The *second* was when he found himself alone with his mother and was able to talk such things over with her.

'No man would ever sin more than four hundred and ninety times a day, would he?' he abruptly asked her on one of these golden occasions.

'What in the world do you mean, Paul? Four hundred and ninety times !'

'Oh, mother,' he replied reproachfully, 'I didn't

suppose you would have forgotten *that*—our very last lesson!'

She asked him to get the Bible and read it to her.

'Here it is, mother,' he cried. ' *"Then came Peter and said, Lord, how often shall my brother sin against me, and I forgive him? till seven times? Jesus saith unto him, I say not unto thee, Until seven times; but, Until seventy times seven."* There, mother, *seventy times seven*—four hundred and ninety times!' cried the boy triumphantly. 'And everybody is sorry some time for his sins, isn't he? Anyway, He said four hundred and ninety times, so that's all right! I guess He'd just forgive the very worstest man in the whole world, wouldn't He, mother?'

'Yes, my boy, always remember *that* as long as you live. Whatever you do, or whatever happens, remember *that!*'

'Sure thing!' cried the boy excitedly. 'I will, mother, certainly! *Seventy times seven! Seventy times seven!* Seventy times seven is four hundred and ninety!'

Mother and boy smiled at each other, and neither of them guessed that, in the adjoining room, the door of which stood open, a distracted and desperate man was standing in silence, drinking in every word. *'Seventy times seven!'* The words, Ralph Connor says, rang like a bell in his soul. He picked up his tobacco-pouch and crept softly away to his studio. Hugh Gaspard—Paul's father—found the manage-

ment of the Pine Croft ranch a strenuous and exact-
ing business, and his art furnished him with a con-
genial and engrossing recreation.   Yet it was not
the worry of the ranch that drove him to his easel
now.   The conversation between his wife and his
boy, to which he had just listened, had thrown him
into a perfect fever of agitation.   But why?

III

Hugh Gaspard's soul was in torture.   It was
stained with a great sin—a sin against God; a sin
against Marion, his wife; a sin against his boy; a
sin against society; a sin against his own people;
and a sin against the red men in the woods.   He
knew that, at that very moment, there sat, up in the
forest near by, a beautiful Indian girl—Onawata,
the daughter of Wahnatahita, the chief of the
Chippewayans—with her baby on her knee.   Had
he not seen her there a few hours earlier?   She had
come many miles to show him her baby, and was
dismayed by the confusion into which her presence
had thrown him.

'Onawata!' he gasped, when he came suddenly
upon her.   'Why have you come?'

'I have made a mistake,' she faltered; 'I did not
know you.   I thought you were a good man.   Why
did you not tell me that you had a woman, a wife?'

For a few minutes, our author tells us, Hugh

stood voiceless before her. He was not a bad man, much less a heartless man. Five years ago, on a hunting trip in the far north land, as the result of an accident, he had made a long stay with a band of Chippewayan Indians, the lords of the Athabasca country. Cared for and nursed back to strength in the wigwam of the chief, he had played the villain, as many another white man had done, without thought of consequence. To-day he stood convicted, appalled, in the presence, not of a squaw who could be easily appeased with gifts and who would think herself very well off were the gifts sufficiently generous, but of a proud young Indian woman, a chief's daughter, exquisitely beautiful in face and form, speaking his own tongue with ease and, in her soft Indian intonation, even with charm. In her arms was *his* child, a fact stubborn, insistent of recognition, with possibility of overwhelming disaster.

Here was the horror that was eating into his heart as he stood there in silence and heard Paul questioning his mother. Within the last twenty-four hours he had peered into the lurid depths of hell. But—seventy times seven is four hundred and ninety! *Seventy times seven!* Forgiveness to the uttermost! Was it—could it be—for *him?* Could God forgive? Could Marion forgive? Could Paul forgive? Could Onawata forgive? Could Wahnatahita forgive?

'Listen!' cried the haughty old chief when he and

Hugh Gaspard at length met, 'listen! You come to my wigwam, wounded, dying. Our people receive you, bring you back from the land of the Great Spirit. For many moons you live with me, my son, her brother! When you grow strong again you become a wolf, you tear my heart; a thief, you rob my cache of the food on which I live; you take my treasure, my pride, my honor, my name! Never again will we look upon your face; never again will you come to our land; the day you come to our land you will die! Go, dog!'

The tall, spare form drawn up to its full height, the outflung command, the dark, eagle-like face, the fiercely blazing eye, the haughty mien, the ringing trumpet-tone; all this, with an acute and damnatory consciousness of baseness and all-too-fully-deserved rebuke, combined to produce upon Hugh's sensitive, artistic soul a truly appalling and overwhelming effect. His whole being shrivelled within him like a growing tree from the blast of a scorching flame.

Seventy times seven is four hundred and ninety! That was the lesson that his wife had urged Paul to remember as long as he lived. But could there be forgiveness for *him*—in this world or in any other? Could God forgive? Could Marion forgive? Could Onawata forgive? Could Paul forgive? Could Wahnatahita forgive? *That* was the question. And the rest of the book is the epic of a great and manifold and wonderful forgiveness.

IV

Marion forgave! At first Hugh dreaded to let her know. She was very frail; the blow might kill her. It did. She made the tragic discovery when visiting the Indian camp, and, like a wounded deer, crept home to die.

'Dead!' cried Hugh, in unutterable anguish, when he arrived at Pine Croft a few days afterwards, 'dead! It's a lie. She wouldn't die without a word to me!' Nor had she.

'She made me promise,' said Paul, stroking his father's cheek, 'she made me promise to tell you about my very last lesson—my Bible lesson, you know.'

'Yes, yes, my boy,' cried poor Hugh eagerly, 'go on, go on!'

'It was about *seventy times seven,* you remember. Forgive unto *seventy times seven!* And she said, "Be sure, be very sure to tell daddy that." She said it was the lesson she loved best in all the Bible.'

Hugh buried his face in his hands. *'Seventy times seven,'* he moaned, *'seventy times seven!* She said that! Oh, my God, my God!' The maid handed him a note that Marion had left for him. There, in poor wandering letters, he read: 'My dear, dear love—I want you so—oh, I want you so! I want to ask you to forgive—to tell you—oh, I want you—with me—now—dear heart——' And then one desperate trailing scrawl, as if death were clutch-

ing at her fingers: *'Remember—*70 x 7*!'*   Then a
poor, faltering 'X.'   'She put her dying lips to it,'
the maid told him.   So greatly had Marion, who
taught her boy the lesson, practised it!

V

Onawata forgave!   In process of time Hugh does
what he can to remove the shame of the proud young
Indian girl by making her his bride, his queen.
And, to the day of his death, she is to him all that
a true wife should be.   But, with the passage of the
years, a bitter and unscrupulous enemy steals into
their lives—a man named Sleeman.   He ruins Hugh;
he attempts to compass the dishonor of Onawata;
and he shadows the career of Paul.   Just once her
hot Indian blood proves too much for Onawata,
and, with a knife in her hand, she all but murders
the man who has darkened their home.   Believing
him to be dead, she flies with her children across the
vast plains of Hudson Bay.   It is a dreadful journey
through blinding blizzards and piled-up snow-drifts;
but Paul insists on sharing her exile with her.   She
dies there, and, on her death-bed, learns that her
knife failed of its deadly work after all.

'Ah, Paul,' she sighs, 'I am glad.   I *was* glad that
he was dead: *now* I am glad that he is alive.   Paul,
I am going!   Perhaps I shall see your father, my
chief.   I cannot go without your word.'   She fumbled

under the pillow and drew out a small parcel, carefully wrapped in deerskin. 'Take it, Paul. It is your mother's good book. You will kiss it and promise that, for her sake, you will not kill this man.' The Bible, which he knew so well, flooded his mind with a rush of sacred memories—the Pine Croft living-room, his mother's face with its wondering tremulous smile as he told her how, up through the tops of the pines, he could see God looking down at him. He remembered how, as she was tucking him in that night, she brought him a new Bible, with his name in it and her name, and, underneath, the beautiful promise that the pure in heart shall see God. She kissed it and she kissed him as she gave it into his hands. The thought of it filled Paul's heart now with uncontrollable emotion. He fell on his knees by Onawata's bedside, gave the promise, and saw her pass in peace.

Even *Wahnatahita* forgave! The most impressive scene in the book is the old chief's visit to his daughter's grave. He proposed at first to take the children with him to be reared in the wigwams; but they all—and especially Singing Water, the little blind girl—clung to Paul.

'It is good,' said the old chief sadly. 'I shall go back to my people with my dead, alone. My heart is cold. Soon the light in my eyes will become night, and in my ears will be no song of the Singing Water.' He grasped Paul's hand, and, accompanied

by his six tall Chippewayan braves, turned silently
homewards.

VI

And, best of all, *God* forgave! On the last Sunday of his life, Hugh Gaspard had attended Communion at the little church, and Paul had accompanied him.   In the process of fencing the tables,
however, the minister had insisted on the necessity
of a forgiving spirit.   'You must forgive him who
wronged you,' he said, 'or you dare not partake.'
As the idea was elaborated and enforced with all the
fervent passion of the minister's Highland soul,
Paul's whole mental horizon became blocked with
one terrible and forbidding object—the face of Sleeman.   The sin of the unforgiving soul daring to
enter into communion with the forgiving Lord was
pressed with relentless logic upon Paul's conscience.
An overwhelming horror fell upon him.   Forgive
Sleeman!   It was unthinkable, intolerable, a moral
impossibility!   Paul rose and slipped out of the
building.   How could he take the bread and the wine
on such conditions?   Hugh, however, kept his seat.
Into *his* heart the rapture of a great forgiveness had
entered, and he was at peace with all the world.
Paul himself returned a few minutes later, the inner
struggle over; and, side by side, father and son took
upon their lips the holy emblems.   A day or two

afterwards Hugh lay on his death-bed, and, with his last breath, extracted from Paul a promise to have mercy upon Sleeman.

VII

Paul achieved great success. He rose to eminence, and all men loved him.

'Paul,' said one of his most intimate friends, to whom he had observed that he was not anxious that Sleeman should suffer, 'Paul, you are a good man— a long way better than I am!'

'I will tell you,' replied Paul, 'why I am able to keep my hands off him, and, perhaps one day, to forgive him. Not yet, not yet; but perhaps one day. That's my mother's chair you are sitting in. And *this,*' he added, rising and going to the sideboard, 'this was her Bible. I am going to read you her last lesson to me.' His companion laid aside his pipe whilst Paul read to him the immortal words which have set for men whose hearts are hot with the passion for vengeance the ideal of the Master of mankind: *'I say not unto thee, Until seven times; but, Until seventy times seven.'*

Then, turning the pages to the story of His crucifixion, he read again: *'Father, forgive them, for they know not what they do.'*

'God knows,' he added, 'I have not yet arrived at that mountain peak. For seven years it has seemed utterly beyond me. But to-night I glimpse it far up in the clouds. *Here* my mother learned to forgive; *here* my father found forgiveness; and *here* I begin to feel how much I need to be forgiven.'

Thus his mother's last lesson—the lesson of the *seventy times seven*—achieved its sublime triumph in the soul of Paul Gaspard. It brought him into fellowship with the Cross; it extracted from his heart all hatred and bitterness; and it imparted to his character such nobleness and sweetness and charm that, wherever he went, his very presence was a benediction.

7

FRANCES WILLARD'S TEXT
1839–1898
American educator and temperance reformer.

Colossians 3:17

I

WITH a spiritual genius that electrified the world, Frances Willard found a way of her own of making history. As Whittier sings:

> She knew the power of banded ill,
> But felt that love was stronger still,
> And organized for doing good
> The world's united womanhood.

On an unforgettable winter's day—'a day unprecedented and unrepeatable'—the Congress of the United States laid aside its regular business and forsook its ordinary functions in order to do honor to the memory of a very illustrious lady. 'For the first time in the history of the Senate,' as the Hon. Shelby M. Cullom put it, 'a day has been set apart that we may talk of a woman.' The State of Illinois had presented Congress with a fine statue of Frances Willard. 'Illinois,' as the Hon. Jonathan Dolliver observed, 'is singularly rich in the treasures of its biography, yet the great commonwealth brings here, with reverence and pride, a work of art so full of gentleness and grace that all the illustrious company about it—the imposing statuary of this noble hall—seems to bow with stately ceremony before the white figure of this elect daughter of Illinois.' One after another, Senators vied with each other in paying tribute to Miss Willard's world-wide and abiding influence. 'Millions of homes are happier for her,' the Hon. Albert J. Beveridge declared, 'millions of wives and mothers bless the thought of her; and countless children have attained to strong, upright, and beautiful maturity who, but for her, would have been for ever soiled and feeble.' So eulogy followed eulogy; and when members of Congress had exhausted the homage of their eloquence, little children came in thousands to bury the pure white statue under an avalanche of fragrant flowers, whilst, for the rest of the day, an interminable procession of women streamed past it, expressing the intensity of their admiration by the silent tribute of their tears.

II

About *Frances Willard's Text* there can be no uncertainty at all. It is inscribed by her own hand on the fly-leaf of her Bible. That marble statue in the Capitol Hall at Washington was unveiled on February 17, 1905. Exactly twenty-eight years earlier—on February 17, 1877—Frances Willard passed through a profound and joyous experience.

Its precise nature is her own secret. But it is evident, from this inscription in her Bible, that the occasion marked a new epoch in her spiritual pilgrimage. She spent the whole day, she tells us, 'in real, joyful, loving study of the kernel of God's word, simply anxious to learn my Father's will.' And then follows this entry:

February 17, 1877.—On this sweet, eventful day in which, with every hour of study, my Bible has grown dearer, I take, as my life-motto henceforth, humbly asking God's grace that I may measure up to it, this wonderful passage from Paul: *'And whatsoever ye do, in word or deed, do all in the name of the Lord Jesus.'*

The name of the Lord Jesus! She is thirty-eight when she makes this entry in her Bible. The work that won for her the gratitude and admiration of mankind is scarcely begun. But she has conceived the idea. She has heard the call. She is about to ride forth, like a new Joan of Arc, on a crusade of lofty conquest. And, before doing so, she solemnly resolves that, *whatever she does, in word or deed, she will do all in the name of the Lord Jesus.* How, I wonder, did that peerless Name obtain such undisputed and unrivalled authority over her? It was not always so. We must regard that February day in 1877 as the central point in her life; and, from that coign of vantage, we must glance *back* over the years behind, and then *forward* into the fruitful years that followed. Let us go *back!*

III

Frances Willard was essentially a child of the
woods, a daughter of the prairies. Her entire girlhood was spent in that romantic home among the
solitudes. It was a picturesque little nest that they
built in that great forest—a cottage with rambling
roof, old-fashioned gables, dormer windows, quaint
little porches, crannies, and out-of-the-way nooks.
To the west was the winding river, serene and broad;
to the east the illimitable prairie, waiting to produce
its golden harvests; to right and left the densely
wooded hills stretching away into infinity. If, in
those gay, careless days, you had paid a surprise
visit to 'Forest Home,' you would probably have discovered the whereabouts of the two sisters by the
sound of their laughter down in the valley, and, on
reaching the spot, you would have found Frances
mounted on her favorite heifer and Mary riding
after her on a goat. In those days the two girls
knew every oriole that flashed through the groves of
hickory, every thrush that sang among the branches
of the oaks, every quail that fluttered through the
stubble, every gopher that peeped shyly from its
hole in the bank, and every squirrel that looked
cheekily down from its home in the tree. Their
father was a born naturalist, ever carrying in his
pocket a selection of tiny implements that would
enable him to take all sorts of observations in the
woods. And, every Sunday afternoon, their mother

would take her girls to her retreat up in the orchard, and, snipping a sprig of fennel or caraway, or pointing to some sweet-faced flower or piping bird or fleecy cloud, would reveal the Soul of Beauty that throbbed behind the World of Being, and would teach the girls to love the Heart at Nature's heart.

Those prairie Sundays were golden days. In later years, Miss Willard loved to linger over the memory of them. 'O those sacred Sabbaths!' she says; 'the early mornings when we ran together through the dewy grass or laid our ears to the brown bosom of the earth to hear her vibrant breathing, to thrill at her pulsing heart! O birds that sang for me, and flowers that bloomed, and mother-love that brooded, and father-love that held! And God's sky over all, and Himself near us everywhere; yes, nearer than near.' When the mother and the girls came in from the orchard, and the family had enjoyed their evening meal in the great farm-kitchen, and the tea-things had been washed and put away, they would all gather in the spacious sitting-room for a delightful evening of music and of song. With tuneful voices they would sing the old, old hymns—sweet in themselves and rich in holiest associations—and nobody suspected that the red-haired little maiden who played the melodeon was being overwhelmed with thoughts that do lie too deep for tears. Yet so it was. Frances always said that her first profound sense of the reality of the spiritual

realm came to her at those Sunday evening sing-
songs on the prairie. Oh, how she longed to be able
to sing those sacred melodies, not only with her lips,
but with her very soul! 'In the sweet summer twi-
lights,' she says, 'it used to just about break my
heart, but not for all the world would I have let anybody know!' The Name—*the name of the Lord
Jesus*—had made its appeal to the ear, the intellect,
the emotions; but it had not yet captivated and sub-
jugated her heart. To her father and her mother
that Name—*the name of the Lord Jesus*—was
everything, literally everything; their faces lit up
whenever they pronounced it; and, in each case, it
was almost the last word that their lips contrived to
frame. But to a faith so simple and so strong
Frances had not yet attained. She was groping
after it. She would lie on the grassy bank of the
river and stretch forth her hand towards the sky.
'If I were God,' she would say to herself, 'if I were
God, and a hand like this were stretched out towards
me, I should have to stoop and clasp it. And I
believe He will, for mother says so!' He did; and
the joy of grasping that divine Hand was the rapture
of her life. But that ecstatic experience came later.
In the meantime the eager young pilgrim had to
tread a stony road.

IV

For Frances was 'the little infidel.' At least, so

they playfully called her. 'My earliest memory,' she says, 'is the memory of my mother sitting, with her Testament in her hand, telling me that it was God's message to me. And instinctively there arose within my spirit the question: How do you know? I was not one who naturally took things for granted. It was intuitive with me to seek for causes and for reasons.' She was for ever startling her parents with her *'How?'* and her *'Why?'* and her *'Please tell me how you know!'* Even when, at the age of nineteen, she left the dear old home on the prairie and became a student at Evanston College, her heart was still a temple of uncertainty. 'I could not say,' she assures us, 'whether there was a God or no; and, if there was, whether He cared for me or not.' The *Whys* and the *Wherefores* were still dominant within her soul. But she was under the spell of great interrogations, not of great negations. She denied nothing. She resented the charge of positive unbelief. When her parents playfully called her their little infidel, she smiled, for she perfectly understood them; but when, later on, she was publicly described as an infidel, and prayers asked on her behalf, she was cut to the very quick. 'They call me an *infidel*,' she cried as, with flaming cheeks and streaming eyes, she threw herself on her bed in a passion of indignation, 'they call me an *infidel;* I consider myself an *inquirer!'*

At about this time some revival meetings were

held, and the president of the college, Professor
W. P. Jones, urged Frances, and some of the more
vivacious girls, to become communicants. Frances
accepted his invitation, but was instantly overcome
by remorse. She felt that she had assumed a false
position. She wrote to the president to express her
regret.

You do not know how hard my heart is [she said]. Three
facts appal me. (1) I am a great sinner; it is a sin greater
than I can comprehend to doubt God and to refuse submission
to Him. (2) I have no excuse for delaying to become a
Christian. (3) I am as cold as an iceberg, as unconcerned as
a stone. If there is a God, a heaven, a hell, a devil, then I
am undone. I have been taught to think that all these exist,
yet from childhood I have doubted. I feel no lack, no want.
If I were to pray quite candidly I should say: 'O God, if
there be a God, save my soul, if I have a soul!'

Here, then, is our brilliant young student of
nineteen! She is severely honest. She is not a
Christian, and she will not pretend that she is one.
She is not an infidel, and she will not allow herself
to be so described. She is full of doubt, but she is
thoroughly ashamed of her doubt. She is still
reaching out her hand to the sky, still hoping to feel
it clasped.

V

Nor has she long to wait. For, at just about
this time, two factors—a gracious friendship and a

serious illness—exercised a potent influence upon her life.

When everybody was condemning poor Frances as an atheist and a sceptic, Mrs. Jones, the wife of Professor Jones, alone met the girl's doubts with sympathy. 'She would come to my room,' Frances says, 'would put her arm around me, would kneel down beside me and pray, with infinite tenderness and yearning, that I might be brought to the point of yielding myself unreservedly to the Saviour, who yielded Himself unreservedly for me. Those bedside talks represented one of the most helpful experiences that I have ever known.'

A few weeks later, in June, 1859, she is stricken down by typhoid fever. Her friends are very anxious, and she knows it. One night, lying in that silent room, a voice seems to plead with her. 'My child,' it says, 'give me thy heart. I have called thee by joy; now I call thee by suffering; but always I call thee because I have loved thee with an everlasting love!'

A long struggle ensues—the struggle between doubt and faith—but at last she solemnly pledges herself that, if she is spared, she will, on her recovery, become a decided Christian.

She recovers; and, one Sunday evening, goes to the Methodist Church. A large congregation has listened to a distinctly commonplace sermon, and seems somewhat impatient for dismissal. Very unexpectedly, however, the minister invites those who may wish to signify their faith in Christ to come forward to the altar. The idea takes everybody by surprise; the revival wave of the previous winter has passed; there is no ripple of religious emotion evident upon the surface of this placid congregation. But, after a moment's pause, one solitary young woman rises from her seat, moves into the aisle, and, with a firm step, walks up to the altar. All eyes converge upon her. There can be no mistaking that face and form! It is Miss Willard, of Evanston College! The effect is electrical. Hundreds of faces, filled with surprise and joy, look into hundreds of others, and many an eye is moist with tears. Some one tremblingly starts the Doxology, and it is sung as if the very stars are expected to join in its joyous melody.

So runs the triumphant record. Beside it let us place two brief entries from Miss Willard's own journal, written at this memorable time.

(1) I have learned to believe in God in terms of Christ Jesus. What Paul says of Christ is what I say: the love John felt it is my dearest wish to cherish.

(2) I shall be twenty years old in September, and I have as yet been of no use in the world.

Moved by these twin impulses—a simple devotion to Christ and a sincere desire to be of use—Frances Willard sets out upon her life-work.

VI

She becomes a teacher. I catch glimpses of her
in her ugly, dismal little school-house, dirty beyond
description, with broken windows, cracked floor, and
the corners cloaked in cobwebs! Sundays and week-
days, she is lonesome to the point of heartbreak, but
her forlorn condition lends a new preciousness to her
faith. She reads her New Testament in solitude and
talks to her children about Jesus. Later, she becomes President of her own old college at Evanston;
and is very proud of her 'beautiful garden of girls.'
Later still, she makes two startling discoveries.
The *first* is that she possesses, in a remarkable
degree, the power of public speech. 'There was,'
says one who heard her frequently, 'a lyric rapture
in her utterance that wrought her hearers into a
delirium of anticipation.' And the *second* discovery
is the discovery of the crowd. 'I saw,' she says, 'the
great unwashed, unkempt, ungospelled, and sin-
scarred multitude.' Like her Lord, she is moved
with compassion. Abandoning her secluded and
academic career, she becomes reformer, evangelist,
philanthropist. Sometimes I see her with Mr.
Moody, sometimes with John B. Gough, sometimes
alone. Sometimes she is moving among the drunk-
ards and the outcasts; sometimes she is pleading
passionately for the closing of the saloons; sometimes she is proclaiming with wonderful winsomeness the love that led Jesus to die. But *whatever she*

does, in word or deed, she does all in the name of the Lord Jesus.

The name of the Lord Jesus! How it grew upon her in charm and sublimity! 'Like a bee,' she says, in one of her last letters, in which she refers to her wide range of reading, 'like a bee that gathers from many fragrant gardens, but flies home to the same friendly and familiar hive, so I gather inspiration from all sources, but fly home to the sweetness and sanctity of the old faith that has been my shelter and solace for so long. Above all things and always, in my mentality and spirituality, I translate God into the terms of *JESUS*. I cannot rest except there!'

A life-size picture of her Lord, presented to her by Lady Henry Somerset, hung near her at the last. As she lay dying, her eyes constantly turned towards it. 'He can do everything for us,' she said. Towards the end she lifted her little, thin, white hand— that active, eloquent hand—and exclaimed exultantly, 'How beautiful to be with God!' They were her last words. Was she thinking, as she raised that worn, white hand of hers, of the day when she lay on the river-bank in the prairie and raised that same hand to the skies? Perhaps! At any rate, she knew on that later day that the hand was clasped, and clasped in the fondness of an eternal caress.

8

HENRY DRUMMOND'S TEXT

1851–1897

Scottish evangelical writer and lecturer.

1 Corinthians 13

I

THE loveliest thing about Henry Drummond was—
Henry Drummond! When Mr. Moody heard of
Drummond's death he said that the prospect of
heaven had become invested with a new charm.
All through his life his friends knew him as 'The
Prince'; and he added lustre to the title by wearing
it. Sir George Adam Smith says that you might
as well attempt to describe a perfume as attempt to
describe Henry Drummond. 'He was,' Ian Maclaren observes, 'a singularly handsome man, such
as you could not match in a ten days' journey, with
delicately cut features, rich auburn hair, and a certain carriage of nobility; but the distinctive and
commanding feature of his face was his eye. It
had a power and hold which were little else than
irresistible and almost supernatural. No man could
be double or base or mean or impure before that
eye.' Those who saw him on some public platform,
wearing with exquisite ease and grace the clothes
that, fitting his fine form most perfectly, imparted to

his general appearance a subtle impression of knight-liness and distinction, and those who met him on the streets of Glasgow, wearing round his shoulders his tartan plaid of green and black, will carry to their graves a memory of extraordinary grace and win-someness.

Nor was his princeliness simply a matter of per-sonal appearance. Dr. Marcus Dods declared that he was the most widely known, the best loved, and the most influential man of his time. 'No man—be he statesman, philosopher, poet, or novelist—was endowed with so distinctive an individuality or wielded so unique an authority as Henry Drum-mond.' No man invading so many realms ever enthroned himself in each with such regal and com-manding authority.

There was scarcely any position that he might not have occupied—and adorned. In point of fact, he was a Presbyterian minister, although he never as-sumed a ministerial title, never wore a ministerial garb, and never accepted a call to a congregation. It would strike one as remarkably odd to hear him referred to as the *Reverend* Henry Drummond. He became Professor of Natural Science; and his lec-tures on scientific themes—now published broadcast —were recognized by the Royal Society, the British Association, and other learned bodies, as being ex-tremely valuable contributions to our knowledge of the subjects that he so skillfully treated. Mr. Glad-

stone tried hard to persuade Drummond to enter
Parliament; Lord Aberdeen, when he went to
Canada as Governor-General in 1893, begged Drum-
mond to accompany him; the McGill University, of
Montreal, did its best to secure him as its principal.
Innumerable were the golden gates that swung open
to invite him.

II

But Henry Drummond cherished in his heart a
radiant secret. He never aspired to exalted office;
he never entangled himself in a multitude of official
duties; he never became, in the ordinary acceptation
of the term, a busy man. There is nothing feverish
or flurried about him; he is never in a whirl or a
flutter; he raises no dust. 'I begin to see,' he writes,
whilst still in his teens, 'I begin to see that the great
thing is to *live* rather than to *work*.' Henry Drummond made history by the choice character that he
developed, and by the beautiful spirit that he so con-
sistently displayed.

His most conspicuous service, as Sir George
Adam Smith points out, was the exhibition of a
Christianity that was perfectly natural. 'You met
him somewhere, a graceful, well-dressed gentleman,
tall and lithe, with a swing in his walk and a brightness on his face, who seemed to carry no cares and
to know neither presumption nor timidity. You

spoke, and found him keen for any of a hundred interests. He fished; he shot; he skated as few can; he played cricket; he would go any distance to see a fire or a football match; and nothing on earth could tear him from a Punch and Judy show. He had a new story, a new puzzle or a new joke every time he met you. Was it on the street? He drew you to watch two messenger-boys meet, grin, knock each other's hats off, lay down their baskets, and enjoy a friendly chaffer of marbles. If it was a rainy afternoon in a country house, he described a new game, and in five minutes everybody was in the thick of it. If it was a children's party, they clamored for his sleight-of-hand. He smoked; he played billiards; and, lounging in the sun, he could be the laziest man you ever saw.' Dr. Robertson Nicoll used to say that Drummond combined, in a wonderful way, the excellences of Robert Louis Stevenson, of Charles Kingsley, and of F. W. Robertson of Brighton. He had Stevenson's gift of fascination and indomitable lightheartedness; he had Kingsley's chivalry and courtesy and passion for humanity; and he had Robertson's early maturity, feminine sensitiveness, and audacious originality.

But we are beating about the bush. This, after all, is not Drummond. There is something more, far more, than all this would suggest—something far more, far deeper, and far sweeter. One story will convey a hint of my meaning. The Rev. D. M.

Ross tells of a poor woman whose husband lay dying. Late one Saturday night she rang the bell at Henry Drummond's door.

'My husband is deein', sir! He's no able to speak to you; and he's no able to hear you; but *I would like him to hae a breath o' you about him afore he dees!'*

III

Now, we shall never discover the hidden secret of this singularly attractive life until we grasp the fact that the roots of his soul struck deeply down into a passage of Scripture. As to *Henry Drummond's Text* we are in no uncertainty at all. He was saturated in it. It simply oozed out of him. It sparkled in his eyes; it shone in his countenance; and, in season and out of season, he expatiated on its splendors. He was never tired of singing its praises.

'I was staying with a party of friends at a country house during my visit to England in 1884,' says Mr. Moody. 'On Sunday evening, as we sat around the fire, they asked me to read and explain some portion of Scripture. Being tired after the services of the day, I told them to ask Henry Drummond, who was one of the party. After some urging, he drew a small Testament from his hip pocket, opened it at the *thirteenth chapter of First Corinthians,* and began to speak on the subject of Love. It seemed to me that I had never heard anything so beautiful, and I determined never to rest until I had brought Henry Drummond to America to deliver that address.'

'Some men,' Mr. Moody adds, writing many years later, 'some men take an occasional journey into the *thirteenth of First Corinthians;* but Henry Drummond was a man who lived there constantly, appropriating its blessings and exemplifying its teachings.'

Henry Drummond repeated that fireside talk all over the world. He could not help it. He was brimming over with its theme. He talked about Paul's Great Hymn of Love in all the principal cities of England and America, and afterwards in Africa, in China, in Japan, and in the South Sea Islands— everywhere! He delivered that address within a few hundred yards of this Australian study of mine. In 1889 it was published. Its sale was phenomenal. Within six months, 185,000 copies were bought up. Since then it has been issued by the million and translated into every European and into many Asiatic languages. When it was translated into German it commanded a greater sale than any German publication of that year. The book brought its astonished author an avalanche of correspondence from all over the world. He had struck a chord that vibrated in every human soul. For the world is dying for love; and Henry Drummond knew it.

IV

His spiritual pilgrimage began early—and characteristically. At the age of nine he attends a little meeting for children, which is held in his uncle Peter's drawing-room. The teacher tells the children the story of the Cross. When the last hymn has been sung, and the others slip out of the room, one boy—a little fellow with curly hair—remains sobbing on the sofa.

'Why, whatever's the matter, Henry?' asks the teacher.

'I'm crying to think that, in spite of all He's done for me, *I don't love Him!*' replies the distressed boy.

The teacher talked with him and prayed with him; and, years afterwards, Henry Drummond told the students of Amherst College that it was at that meeting in his uncle's home that his Christian life began. 'It was then,' he said, 'that I first began to love the Saviour.'

The phraseology employed in the telling of this simple tale is intensely significant.

'I do not *love* Him!' sobs the boy of nine.

'It was then that I began to *love* Him!' exclaims the teacher to whom the whole world is listening.

'The real secret of his charm,' says Sir William Robertson Nicoll, 'lay in his passionate devotion to Jesus Christ.' Henry Drummond really loved his Lord; loved Him naturally, intensely, increasingly. He lavished upon his Saviour a vast wealth of deep, strong, masculine tenderness. A woman who was applying for her Communion token at Dundee ex-

plained the work of grace in her soul by saying that
she once heard Mr. McCheyne exclaim in prayer,
'*O Lord, Thou knowest that we love Thee!*' and she
could see by his shining face that he meant it. Henry
Drummond affected men very similarly. He made
them feel that, unless they cherished a real fondness
for Christ, and had entered into the intimate friendship of the Son of God, they were missing life's best.

'Love is everything!' he exclaims, in his eloquent
exposition of his text. 'Love is life; to *love* abundantly is to *live* for ever. Why do you want to live
to-morrow? It is because there is someone who
loves you, and whom you want to see, and be with,
and love back. It is when a man has no one to love
him that he commits suicide. Be it but the love of a
dog, it will keep him in life; but let *that* go, and he
has no contact with life, no reason to live. The
energy of life has failed.' Then, lifting his argu-
ment on to the highest plane, he insists that eternal
life can only rest in an eternal love; and how can
there be an eternal love save in the love of the
Eternal?

V

This is his message, and he delivers it wherever he
goes. At the invitation of the Duke and Duchess of
Westminster, he conducts a series of meetings in the
ballroom of Grosvenor House. On one occasion we

see present Lord Selborne, the Marquis of Harting-
ton, Lord Sherbrooke, the Right Hon. W. E.
Forster, M.P., the Right Hon. H. C. E. Childers,
M.P., and hundreds of others scarcely less distinguished. On another occasion, the meeting is attended by Lord Aberdeen, Mr. (afterwards Lord)
Balfour, Mr. (afterwards Lord) Curzon, Dr. J. E.
Welldon, head master of Harrow, Captain John Sin-
clair, M.P., and a host of similar celebrities. 'The
great square room'—so runs the newspaper report—
'was densely crowded by an interested and representative gathering—politicians, doctors, authors,
artists, critics, soldiers, and barristers, many of them
of the highest distinction, together with a large
sprinkling of smart young society men whose appearance would scarcely have suggested a vivid interest
in spiritual concerns. On everybody present, however, the effect produced was the same; and the audience departed profoundly impressed by the words
of wisdom and solemnity issuing from the lips of
this remarkably equipped and remarkably well-
dressed young man.' With simple eloquence he
talked about Love—the Love that beareth all things,
believeth all things, hopeth all things, endureth all
things—the Love of God to man—the Love of man
to God—the Love of man to his brother—the Love
that is the Greatest Thing in the World. *'Now
abideth Faith, Hope, Love; these three; but the
greatest of these is Love.'* And, when his address

was finished, he asked his distinguished audience to bow with him in supplication.

'Lord Jesus,' he prayed, 'we have been talking to one another about Thee; now we talk to Thee face to face. Bless all here who love Thee in sincerity. Help those who love Thee not, and who miss Thee every day they live, here and now to begin their attachment and devotion to Thy Person and service; for Thy name's sake. Amen.'

Love!
The love that is life!
Bless all who love!
Help those who love Thee not, to love Thee!

That was ever the burden of Henry Drummond. Even his scientific books are full of it. In the *Ascent of Man* he devotes three whole chapters to his favorite theme. He calls them: 'The Struggle for the Life of Others,' 'The Evolution of a Mother,' and 'The Evolution of a Father.' But it is all about Love. The history of life upon this planet is, he maintains, a stately and impressive love-story. Love, he argues in every paragraph, love is joy; love is light; love is life; love is everything!

No man ever addressed such a variety of audiences as Henry Drummond. He preaches in pulpits; he lectures before the great scientific assemblies; he joins Mr. Moody in pleading with the immense crowds that gather to hear the American evangelists. He is equally at home among public school boys, university students, bootblacks, crossing-sweepers, African negroes, South Sea Islanders, London stockbrokers, Australian squatters, peers of the realm, leaders of society, princes of commerce, captains of industry, doctors, lawyers, scientists, and men of every class and kind.

But the audience that he loved best, and the audience with which his plea was most effective, was an audience of *one*. Henry Drummond was a Prince of Buttonholers. He was often to be seen going home through the streets at dead of night with a man in whose arm his own was linked. Sometimes his companion was a well-known citizen; sometimes an ordinary ne'er-do-well; and he was specially happy when he found that he had chummed up with an oddity of some kind. The unconventional, the Bohemian, and the vagrant were his peculiar delight. Showmen of all sorts were an infinite joy to him. A Spanish guitar-player, a laddie who performed on the penny whistle, a music-hall singer, a cornet-player; in such society he simply revelled. 'To draw souls one by one,' he used to say, 'to woo their confidence and steal from them the secret of their lives, to talk them clean out of themselves, to read them off like a page of print, to pervade them with one's own spiritual essence and make them transparent— *this* is the secret of all true success.' And he became a past-master in the art. He made every man he tackled feel that he loved him. And he made his companion *feel* that he loved him for the simple reason that *he really did.*

VI

For love—the love that is glorified in that noble chapter in which, according to Mr. Moody, Henry Drummond made his home—was the master-motive, the supreme dynamic, of Henry Drummond's life. In that famous address which he was so fond of delivering he says that Paul 'passed this thing, Love, through the prism of his inspired intellect, and it comes out on the other side broken up into its elements.' Thus analysed, it has nine ingredients:

Patience—'Love suffereth long.'

Kindness—'And is kind.'

Generosity—'Love envieth not.'

Humility—'Love vaunteth not itself, is not puffed up.'

Courtesy—'Doth not behave itself unseemly.'

Unselfishness—'Seeketh not her own.'

Good Temper—'Is not easily provoked.'

Guilelessness—'Thinketh no evil.'

Sincerity—'Rejoiceth not in iniquity, but rejoiceth in the truth.'

'As I examine this analysis,' says Mr. Moody, 'I remember that all these ingredients were interwoven into Henry Drummond's daily life, making him the most lovable man I have ever known. Was it

Courtesy you looked for? he was a perfect gentleman. Was it Kindness? he was always preferring another. Was it Humility? he was the essence of simplicity. It could be truthfully said of him, as of the early apostles, that men took knowledge of him that he had been with Jesus.'

Nathaniel Hawthorne tells the story of the boy who gazed so long and so admiringly upon the Great Stone Face—the noble face cut in the chalk hill near his home—that, little by little, his own face took on the features of the face that he so fondly contemplated, and, when he grew to manhood, his companions saw that the face carved on the hill was his own! Similarly, Henry Drummond gazed so constantly and so intently and so fondly upon *the thirteenth chapter of the First Epistle to the Corinthians* that he became its very expression and embodiment. He lived in that chapter, to quote Mr. Moody's phrase once more; he made his home there; grew familiar with every nook and corner in it; learned to love each room and corridor and passage; and, as a natural consequence, he bore the choice fragrance and the beautiful spirit of the place into all the dusty highways and by-ways of the ordinary, work-a-day world.

9

TOM BROWN'S TEXT

Main character in *Tom Brown's Schooldays* by Thomas Hughes.

Luke 18:13

I

A BOY is a boy. You cannot classify him. He
belongs to a genus of his own. He has ways of his
own; sensations of his own; ideas of his own. He is
compounded of a thousand qualities so oddly as-
sorted and so incongruously mingled that it seems
impossible that they can be harmoniously blended
within the narrow compass of a single personality.
He whimpers like a baby, yet swaggers like a prince.
He is fearless as a lion, yet timid as a hare. He is
honest as the noonday, yet deceitful as the twilight.
He is so angelically good that you sometimes fancy
you perceive an embryo halo encircling his innocent
brow; and yet, at the same time, he is so audaciously
and outrageously wicked that you are tortured by
hideous anticipations of a felon's cell and a hang-
man's rope. He is compounded of considerable
quantities of Essence of Paradise liberally infused
with Tincture of Perdition. There is nothing in
the heavens above nor on the earth beneath to be
compared with him. He belongs, as I say, to a
class of his own. And, just because he has ways of
his own, sensations of his own, and ideas of his own,
he has a religion of his own. It is not his father's

religion, nor his grandfather's; it is not his mother's
religion, nor his grandmother's. It is inherently
and essentially *his* religion. It would not fit his
father or his grandfather, any more than their religion would fit him. Still less would it fit his mother
or his grandmother. It is fundamentally a boy's
religion. And by far the best exposition of a boy's
religion that has ever been committed to paper is to
be found in the stirring pages of *Tom Brown's
Schooldays.*

'It's the jolliest tale ever told,' wrote Kingsley to
the author, many years after its publication; 'isn't
it a comfort to your old bones to have written such
a book?' It certainly was; and for many reasons.
And conspicuously among those reasons stands the
fact that whilst, with almost brutal frankness, the
story portrays the life of a schoolboy on its rougher
and wilder side, it nevertheless makes it clear to
those who read between the lines that, at certain
vulnerable points, a boy is remarkably susceptible,
extraordinarily impressionable, and singularly sensitive to the approach of spiritual suggestions. On
one side of his complex nature he appears to be as
rigid as steel, as hard as granite, and as inflexible
as adamant; on another side—the side that he carefully conceals from public view—he is as flexible as
silk, as pliable as wax, and as plastic as clay in the
hands of the potter. And here, deftly limned in the
pages of Thomas Hughes's immortal classic, I trace

the outlines of those subtle forces by which the soul
of a boy may be influenced and molded.

II

A boy is a born hero-worshipper. He readily falls
under the spell of a lofty and noble character. That,
primarily and emphatically, is the message of *Tom
Brown's Schooldays*. It is a story of Rugby and
Arnold—especially Arnold. For in those days, as
somebody has finely said, Rugby *was* Arnold, and
Arnold was Rugby. Into the lives of these boys
there strode a handsome, gallant, indomitable figure,
who, by the pure knightliness of his bearing, by the
quiet sway of his princely authority, and by the
sheer magnetism of his captivating personality,
compelled every boy at Rugby to love, worship, and
obey him.

And no wonder! For it is not too much to say
that the history of the public schools of England
divides itself into two parts—before Arnold and
after. In the early part of the nineteenth century
everybody lamented that the condition of the great
schools was an open scandal; yet nobody saw any
way of effecting their reform. It was just when the
situation was becoming desperate that Dr. Arnold,
at the age of thirty-two, was appointed headmaster
of Rugby. He had already made his mark, and
there were those who viewed with profound disap-
pointment·his acceptance of his new position. 'What

a shame,' they said, 'that a man cut out for a Prime Minister should spend his life in teaching school-boys!' But Arnold felt very differently. He saw the crying need of the hour, and to him that need was a clarion call, a taunt, a challenge! He entered upon his new duties with a high and dauntless spirit; and, ignoring influential opposition and pitiless criti-cism, began to give effect to his ideals. As Dean Stanley says, few scenes on record are more char-acteristic of him than that in which we see him reluctantly yet unhesitatingly expelling a number of boys from the school. In the midst of the storm of angry discontent which his action immediately excited, Arnold stood like a rock on which the waves were vainly beating.

'Gentlemen,' he said, as he calmly rose and faced the school, 'it is not necessary that Rugby should be a school of three hundred, or one hundred, or even fifty boys; but it *is* necessary that it should be a school of Christian gentlemen!' From that day he was master, not only in name, but in fact; he was enthroned; his authority was absolute. His spirit pervaded everything. 'His very presence,' as one of his boys afterwards confessed, 'his very presence seemed to create a new spring of health and vigor within us, and to give to life an interest and an ele-vation which remained with us long after we had left him. Indeed, he dwelt so continually in our thoughts, as a living and commanding influence,

that, even when death had taken him from us, the
bond appeared to be still unbroken, and the sense of
separation was almost lost in the still deeper sense of
a life and a union indestructible.'   The pages of
Stanley's noble biography are enriched by many such
tributes; yet it is not to the biography that we turn
when we wish to gaze upon a life-sized and life-like
portrait of the world's greatest headmaster.

Mr. Justice Hughes was never tired of telling why
he wrote *Tom Brown's Schooldays*.   He was thirty-
three at the time.   His youth and early manhood had
been dominated by the spirit of the old school—by
Rugby—Arnold's Rugby.   Arnold had died in 1842,
at the age of forty-seven, Hughes being then in his
teens.   Two years later, Stanley's *Life of Arnold*
was published.   But, although that volume is in
some respects one of the best biographies in the language, Hughes felt—as many of Arnold's old boys
felt—that it failed to convey to the ordinary reader
a vivid and realistic impression of the Rugby atmosphere.   It was all about Arnold; and yet, somehow,
the Arnold that they knew was not there.   Instead
of evaporating, this uncomfortable conviction deepened with the years, and at last Hughes could hold
his hand no longer.   One summer's evening in 1856
—fourteen years after Arnold's death—he found
himself chatting with a few of his old schoolfellows.
'I have often thought,' he said, 'that the doctor
might be made to live again in a lively novel for

schoolboys, not stilted and pedantic like *Sandford and Merton,* but written in a rollicking spirit, full of snap and vim!' He set to work, and, before long, found himself inditing a letter to Alexander Macmillan, the publisher. 'I always told you,' he says, 'that I would write a book that would make your fortune; and, surely enough, I've done it! I've gone and written a one-volume novel for boys. It concerns Rugby in Arnold's time.' Hughes meant the note as a joke; but it proved prophetic. The manuscript was a gold-mine for Macmillans. In thirty years the book romped through sixty-six editions; and it is impossible to compute the circulation that it has since enjoyed.

And so, thanks to *Tom Brown's Schooldays,* we have all capitulated to the charm of Arnold. With Tom Brown, we have seen the illustrious dominie on the cricket ground; in the lanes round Rugby; amidst the felicities of that home which Arnold himself said seemed to be *too* happy; in the class-rooms; and in that familiar chapel that Arnold has made famous for all time. For, as the novelist says, 'the great event in Tom's life—as in every Rugby boy's life of that day—was the first sermon from the doctor. The oak pulpit standing out by itself above the school seats; the tall, gallant form; the kindling eye; the voice, now soft as the low notes of a flute, now clear and stirring as the call of the light infantry bugle; and the long lines of young faces rising tier

above tier down the long length of the chapel, from
the little boy's who had just left his mother to the
young man's who, next week, was going out into the
great world rejoicing in his strength; all this made
up a great and solemn spectacle, and never more so
than on those occasions when the only lights were in
the pulpit, and the soft twilight stole over the rest
of the chapel, deepening into darkness in the high
gallery behind the organ.'   At such moments Arnold
seemed to his boys, not a prince only, but a prophet
—a prophet of culture, but a prophet of passionate
and persuasive eloquence.   'He taught us,' says
Hughes, 'that, in this wonderful world, no boy can
tell which of his actions is indifferent and which
not.   He taught us that, by a thoughtless word or
look, we may lead astray a brother for whom Christ
died.   He taught us that a boy's only safety and only
wisdom lies in bringing the whole life into obedience
to Him who made us for Himself and redeemed us
with His own most precious blood.'

Is it any wonder that so kingly a man held the
hearts of his boys in the hollow of his hand?   When,
in 1842, the news ran through the country that
Arnold of Rugby had died suddenly of heart disease,
it did not create the public sensation that marks the
death of a distinguished soldier or an eminent statesman.   But, scattered over the land, there were a few
hundred young men who, when they heard the news,
turned pale and betrayed the deepest emotion.   Tom

Brown was fishing in a Scottish stream when a companion, sitting on the grassy bank, read out the tragic paragraph. 'Tom's hand stopped half-way in his cast; his line and flies went all tangling round and round his rod; you might have knocked him down with a feather.' He abandoned the holiday at once, and set out for Rugby. The passage with which the book closes—the passage that describes Tom offering the homage of his grief at the doctor's tomb in the old chapel—is one of the most affecting in our literature.

III

The second part of *Tom Brown's Schooldays* opens with the story of Tom's conversion. 'The turning-point in our hero's career had now come,' says the author, 'and the manner of it was as follows.' Tom's conversion is not the sort of conversion that one finds in the evangelical records: but it is a schoolboy conversion. And a schoolboy, who has ways of his own, and sensations of his own, and ideas of his own, is entitled to a conversion peculiarly his own. Very appropriately, this section of the book is headed by Lowell's lines:

Once to every man and nation comes the moment to decide,
In the strife of Truth with Falsehood, for the good or evil
    side:
Then it is the brave man chooses, while the coward stands
    aside,
Doubting in his abject spirit, till his Lord is crucified.

A boy knows only one virtue. I have a boy of my own—a little fellow of ten—who loves at odd moments to steal into this quiet study of mine. He darts straight across to the bookcase that contains the biographies. And, reading aloud the names, he asks one crucial question: 'Was he a very *brave* man?' He never inquires as to whether the subject of the biography was a *good* man or a *clever* man or a *successful* man. To a boy there is only one test. Was he *brave?* Courage is the only flower that is ever coveted for a boy's garden.

Now, the grace of courage unfolded itself to Tom Brown's eyes in a totally unexpected form. The chapter that tells of Tom's conversion is the chapter that describes the coming of Arthur to Rugby. Arthur was a slight, pale boy, with large blue eyes and light fair hair, who seemed ready to shrink through the floor. He was a quivering little bundle of nerves; he looked as if a puff of wind would blow him away. He had been coddled by his mother and his sisters down in his Devonshire home. When his box was opened, his schoolfellows discovered, to their intense amazement and boisterous derision, some pretty little night-caps, most beautifully and tastefully made. 'The kind mother and sisters, who sewed that delicate stitching with aching hearts, little thought of the trouble they might be bringing on the young head for which they were meant.' At Dr.

Arnold's request, Tom took the frail little fellow under his wing, and Arthur looked up to his new protector with eyes of adoring gratitude.

Poor little Arthur! As the first day, with all its new and distressing experiences, dragged itself on, he turned appealingly to Tom again and again.

'Please, Brown, may I wash my face and hands?' All day long it was: 'May I do this?' 'May I do that?' But at night, in the dormitory, he did a thing for which he asked nobody's permission. Tom was sitting at the bottom of his own bed unlacing his boots. His back was towards Arthur, so that he did not see what was happening. Several of the boys had already tumbled into bed.

'The light burned clear; the noise went on. It was a trying moment for the poor little lonely boy. But, without asking Tom whether or not he might do it, he dropped on his knees by his bedside, as he had done from earliest childhood, to open his heart to Him who hears the cry alike of the tender child and of the strong man in his agony.'

There was a general titter. Several of the boys burst into open laughter. One big, brutal fellow picked up a slipper and threw it at the kneeling boy, calling him a snivelling young shaver. Tom turned; saw the whole; and in a moment the boot that he had just pulled from his foot flew straight at the head of the bully, who had barely time to throw up his arm and catch it on his elbow.

'Confound you, Brown, what do you mean?' he roared.

'Never mind what I mean,' replied Tom, every drop of his blood tingling. 'If any fellow wants the other boot, he knows how to get it!'

That night Tom could not sleep. His head throbbed; his heart leapt; he remembered the promises that *he* had made to his own mother; he lay in bed and cried as if his heart would break. He was a coward! Yes, the vice that, of all others, he had most loathed and despised, was sheeted home and burned in to his own soul! At last he reached a high resolve, and then, but not till then, he fell asleep.

'Next morning'—so runs the record—'Tom rose, washed, and dressed, and then, in the face of the whole room, knelt down to pray! But what to say? He was conscious that all eyes were upon him. At last, from his inmost heart, a still, small voice seemed to breathe forth the words of the publican: *"God be merciful to me, a sinner!"* He repeated them over and over, clinging to them as for his life. He then rose from his knees comforted and humbled and ready to face the whole world. It was not needed, however. Two other boys besides Arthur had already followed his example, and thus Tom learned that *he who has conquered his own coward spirit has conquered the whole world.'*

This, briefly, is the story of Tom's conversion. In

a sense, it was the conversion of Rugby; for Mr. Hughes says that, after Tom took his stand, the school became a better place for everybody.

VI

There is yet another phase in the spiritual history of Tom Brown. It occurs when Arthur, in the course of his terrible illness, catches the vision of the glory of service, and, on his recovery, tells Tom of the wonders he has seen. Heaven itself was opened to the sick boy, and, as he gazed upon its splendors, he saw that everybody was working! *Everybody!* The vision greatly comforted Arthur by showing him that the Great Master had some work that even *he,* with his puny strength, could undertake. It was with a pale face, but with sparkling eyes, that he told Tom of that wonderful experience. And Tom listened breathless, spellbound, and profoundly impressed.

But this was later. Yet it is the natural and inevitable sequel. He who, in an agony of penitence like Tom's, has cried from the depths of his soul: *'God be merciful to me, a sinner,'* will soon hear a Voice and catch a Vision that will set his brain planning and his hands toiling for the redemption of the whole wide world.

10

JOHN MILTON'S TEXT
1608–1674

English poet and author of *Paradise Lost.*

Psalm 107:1; 118:1

I

IT was in the late hours of a bleak November Sunday night, with the rain lashing at the window-panes and the wind howling in the chimney, that the purest and most majestic of all our English minstrels laid aside for ever the lyre from which he had poured such deathless harmonies. Poor blind John Milton! We all seem to have watched him as, with seraphic face, he dictates to one or other of his daughters the glowing stanzas that have made his name immortal. Clad in his suit of coarse grey cloth, he sits, in summer-time, among the sweet-smelling flowers of his well-kept garden; whilst, in winter-time, garbed in black velvet, he imprisons himself in his dreary chamber, hung with its rusty green tapestry, and wings his inspired fancy on its most audacious flights. His rich auburn hair, which retained something of its gold to the last, falls over his slightly stooping shoulders, setting off a face remarkable for its sweetness, its strength, and its serenity. His soft grey eyes give no hint of their sad, sad secret.

II

Very seldom has a man set himself as deliberately as did Milton to a colossal task, and, with so little encouragement, carried it to its completion. He was a callow youth when he conceived the stupendous project; he was an old man when he rolled up the finished manuscript. In the interval he travelled far, learned much, and became engrossed in many cares. But the dream of his boyhood was never forgotten. Like the Temple, erected without beat of hammer or clink of trowel, the glorious work was silently growing in the poet's soul. He brooded upon it in secret; his masterpiece was always there at the back of his mind.

'You ask me,' he writes, as a young fellow in the twenties, 'you ask me what I am thinking about? Why, with God's help, of *immortality!* Forgive the word; I only whisper it in your ear! Yes, I am pluming my wings for a flight!'

He felt that there was no hurry; he allowed his earliest conceptions to simmer in his mind; he exposed his plastic fancy to the moulding influence of great events. And a moment's reflection will show that the events of his time were by no means destitute of impressiveness and grandeur. He was only seven when Shakespeare died; he was ten when Sir Walter Raleigh was executed; he was twelve when the *Mayflower* sailed. His youthful enthusiasms were awakened by the tumult of thought that swept

the scientific world as a result of the sensational discoveries of Harvey and Kepler.   Much of *Paradise
Lost* was written whilst London was being decimated by the Great Plague; and it was amidst the
charred ruins of the metropolis that he handed the
manuscript to his publisher.   He lived through the
whole of the Civil War; he mingled freely with the
principal actors in those stormy and dramatic scenes;
he saw the rise and fall of the Commonwealth, the
execution of the King, and the death of Cromwell.
The pulsations of such momentous happenings
stirred the deepest emotions of a singularly sensitive
and impressionable spirit; they inscribed themselves
indelibly upon his memory; and, taking to themselves weird and fantastic shapes, they wove themselves into the splendid fabric of his priceless epic.

III

For there is more of worldly wisdom and of
human life in Milton's poetry than even his admirers have been wont to recognize.   Did not
Napoleon tell Sir Colin Campbell that he stole the
strategy of Austerlitz, holus-bolus, from the sixth
book of *Paradise Lost?*   The poem reads like the
story of a war among archangels; as a matter of
fact, it is the story of a war among Englishmen.
Milton was a Puritan; in many respects the choicest
of the Puritans.   Green regards him as not only the

highest, but the completest, type of Puritanism. He represents Puritanism at its very best. In the Puritanism of Milton there is nothing ascetic, nothing intolerant, nothing hypocritical, nothing bitter. To him, England, under the sway of the Puritans, was Paradise. But he lived to witness the great reaction, and his poem is the epic of a lost cause. There came a time, to quote Macaulay's stinging sentences, 'there came days, never to be recalled without a blush, the days of servitude without loyalty, and sensuality without love, of dwarfish talents and gigantic vices, the paradise of cold hearts and narrow minds, the golden age of the coward, the bigot, and the slave. The caresses of harlots and the jests of buffoons regulated the policy of the State.' And so on; England was knee-deep in mire. Here stood the tragedy of Milton's life; and, but for it, *Paradise Lost* could never have been written. Superficial critics have deplored the years that Milton devoted to political pursuits; they forgot that it was his ardent patriotism that drove him into politics, and that, by that selfsame patriotism, his sublimest poetry was inspired. In John Milton three distinct elements are to be found inextricably intermingled—his piety, his patriotism, and his poetry; and he who would penetrate and appreciate the remote and elusive personality of John Milton must take the trouble to trace those three separate streams to their common fountain-head.

IV

And, as all the authorities bear witness, the source of those three streams is to be found in the Scriptures. John Milton was a tremendous lover of the Bible. He used to say that, if England became a Bible-reading, Bible-believing, Bible-studying nation, its distresses would quickly vanish and its wounds be healed. Other classical writers have been fired by illustrious literary precedents of many kinds; but it is no exaggeration to say that Milton drew the whole of his inspiration from the Bible. And no wonder! For, during the most impressionable years of his life, his character was moulded by the hands of three men; and all three of them regarded the Bible as earth's chiefest treasure.

The *first* of the three was his father. We possess a charming picture of the happy home in Bread Street, Cheapside, afterwards destroyed by the Great Fire. The elder Milton had two passions—his passion for the Bible and his passion for music. Every evening, the day's work done, the whole family would gather—the father sitting on one side of the hearth; the mother on the other; the eldest girl and her brother John at the table; and little Kit sprawling in front of the fire—and together they would read, and discuss with animation, some interesting passage of Scripture, and would join in singing heartily several of the Psalms. 'And thus,' as Dr. Masson observes in his six-volume biography of

Milton, 'and thus a disposition towards the serious, a regard for religion as a chief concern in life, and a dutiful love of the parents who so taught him, would be cultivated in Milton from his earliest years. Happy child to have such parents! Happy parents to have such a child!' It was the joy of the elder Milton's declining days that John—then a youth of twenty-nine—abode beneath the parental roof; and, when the old man died, his Bible and music-books lay open on the table beside his bed.

The *second* of the three men was the Rev. Richard Stokes, the minister of the parish of All-Hallows, Bread Street. Mr. Stokes was a man of fine personality and of intense evangelistic fervor; no man in London was more highly esteemed than he. He labored night and day for the spiritual welfare of the citizens, and especially of those of his own parish. He seldom left his own pulpit; and he rejoiced as much over the conversion of a soul as some men would rejoice over the discovery of a gold-mine or the conquest of a kingdom. He had a special fondness for young people, and was singularly skilful in arresting their attention and winning their confidence. Mr. Stokes knew his Bible as few ministers knew it; he constantly referred to it in terms of enthusiasm and endearment; and every word that fell from the good man's lips increased John's affection for the sacred volume which his father had taught him to cherish.

The *third* of the trio was his tutor, Thomas Young, a sturdy Scot, who left upon John, in addition to the impress of his excellent character, some of the oddities of his Northern speech. To the last day of his life Milton rolled his *r's* like a true-born Scotsman. Mr. Young read the Scriptures, in the original tongues, with his young pupil every morning. Three years afterwards—John being then at Cambridge—I find him writing to his old tutor, thanking him for the gift of a Hebrew Bible. 'I call God to witness,' he says, 'how much as a father I regard you. Out of my vehement affection for you I always fancy you with me, and speak to you, and endeavor to behave as though you were actually present.'

Later on, Mr. Young was banished for his faith. John writes to him, expressing his whole-hearted sympathy and unalterable affection. He can imagine him, he says, languishing on alien soil, but turning the pages of his beloved Bible and drawing rich streams of comfort from that source. 'Take courage,' he writes in conclusion; 'Elijah had to live for awhile in the desert; Paul had to flee for his life; and Christ Himself left the country of the Gergesenes! God will protect you in the midst of danger and bring you back to the joys of your native land!'

These three men implanted in the heart of John Milton an affection for the Bible which deepened with the years. If John Wesley took the whole world for his parish, John Milton took the whole Bible as his text. It is eminently characteristic of him, for he who deals with Milton is 'splashing on a ten-league canvas with brushes of comet's hair.' If it be objected that the Bible is too comprehensive to be regarded as *John Milton's Text,* we could moderate its immensity by saying that the Psalms represent *John Milton's Text.* For, as Mr. Prothero points out, the Psalms threw a singularly potent spell over the life of Milton, and he applied some of his best powers to the task of paraphrasing them. Or, if the text is still too bewildering, we could reduce it to a sentence: '*O give thanks unto the Lord; for He is good; for His mercy endureth for ever.*' Milton loved those words, and, at the age of fifteen, expressed their message in verses that now find a place in all our hymn-books:

> Let us with a gladsome mind
> Praise the Lord, for He is kind:
>   For His mercies aye endure,
>   Ever faithful, ever sure.

Mark Pattison has shown that the subtle secret of the superb strength of *Paradise Lost* lies in the fact that Milton never knew the shadow of a doubt as to the divine authority of the Scriptures. He accepted them unwaveringly; based all his hope on the revelation which they unfolded to him; and, saturated with their thought and spirit, he conceived his masterpiece.

Nobody can read *Paradise Lost* without feeling that Milton had implicit faith in the Bible. He loved it for its own sake; he gloried in it as a sublime revelation of the love of God to men; he rested with childlike simplicity on the redemptive efficacy of the atoning Cross. One of his earliest Odes is addressed to the divine Babe at Bethlehem; another is offered to the Saviour in the hour of His agony. And Milton anticipated, with the most serene confidence, the ultimate triumph of the Crucified.

Come forth out of Thy royal chambers, O Prince of all the Kings of the Earth [he prays]; put on the visible robes of Thy Imperial Majesty; take up that unlimited sceptre which Thy Almighty Father hath given Thee; for now the voice of Thy bride calls Thee, and all creatures sigh to be renewed!

Milton, making a companion of his Bible, became infected by its unconquerable hope. In the depth of winter he heard the songs of a coming spring; in the darkest night he heard the heralds of the dawn.

V

In recognizing the inestimable service rendered to Milton, and to the world, by these three good men— his father, his minister, and his tutor—would it seem ungrateful to regret that Milton's training was so exclusively masculine? No woman was permitted to take a hand in it. And was it on this account, I wonder, that the poor young poet was thrust out

into life handicapped by a total incapacity for understanding women? Who can read the pitiful record
of his quixotic adventures in the realm of matri-
mony save to the accompaniment of smiles and
tears? And, in *Paradise Lost*, the least convincing
character is Eve. When Milton sings of archangels,
or even of fiends, he is positively sublime; but when
he attempts to describe a woman he is clearly out of
his depth.

Partly on this account, John Milton was the lone-
liest man of his time, just as, through all the ages, he
takes his place as the most solitary figure in either
history or fiction. He stands altogether detached,
an arresting and pathetic personality. Nobody
understood him; nobody shared his aspirations;
nobody showed him the slightest sympathy. 'He
dwelt apart,' as Wordsworth puts it in his fine apos-
trophe:

> Thy soul was like a star and dwelt apart;
>   Thou hadst a voice whose sound was like the sea;
>   Pure as the naked heavens, majestic, free,
> So didst thou travel on life's common way.

He married three times; and each of his wives
regarded his insatiable penchant for composition as
a tiresome mania. Even his daughters felt the bore-
dom of his everlasting dictation to be almost intolerable. When, at last, his ponderous manuscript was
complete, nobody saw anything in it. Pitying his

sightlessness, an enterprising publisher gave him five pounds for the copyright, promising another five if, by any strange chance, the work reached a second edition. On the appearance of the poem, the critics surveyed the vast array of incomprehensible stanzas and shook their heads. Edmund Waller, the poet, was then in the hey-day of his popularity. 'The old schoolmaster, John Milton,' wrote Waller, 'hath published a tedious poem on the Fall of Man; if its length be not considered a merit, it hath no other.' But John Milton was not writing for the likes of Edmund Waller. Mark Rutherford declares that, a thousand years hence, a much better estimate of Milton will be possible than that which can be formed to-day. John Milton had a tryst to keep with the immortals; and it mattered little to him what the seventeenth century had to say about that particular tryst.

During three momentous centuries, Milton has slowly but surely grown upon the imaginations of men. He is more reverenced every year. To tear him from our annals and traditions would be to create an aching void that could never, by any possibility, be filled. 'Never,' as Dr. Garnett once said, 'never before nor since, has such a splendid figure crossed the broad stage of English life.' He stands, and ever must stand, as the embodiment of all that is best in our national spirit. As George Meredith sings:

                     Were England sunk
          Beneath the shifting tides, her heart, her brain,
          The smile she wears, the faith she holds, her best
          Would live full-toned in the grand delivery
          Of his cathedral speech; an utterance
          Almost divine, and such as Hellespont,
          Crashing its breakers under Ida's frown,
          Inspired; yet worthier he whose instrument
          Was by comparison the coarse reed-pipe;
          Whereof have come the marvellous harmonies,
          Which, with his lofty theme, of infinite range,
          Abash, entrance, exalt.

There are men who stand aside from the period which happens to give them birth. Their genius is disconcerting, majestic, terrifying. The world holds aloof from them. They are the citizens, not of an age, but of the ages. And the ages, quick to identify their own, hail them, applaud them, crown them. Of such pure and deathless spirits, John Milton is the supreme and peerless representative.

11

ADONIRAM JUDSON'S TEXT

1788–1850

American missionary to Burma.

Ephesians 3:17–18

I

HE is a thorough-paced sceptic, this dashing young fellow with the slight and fragile frame, the round and rosy face, the laughing brown eyes, and the rich shock of chestnut hair. There is something defiant about his unbelief. He is the son of a Congregational minister in Massachusetts, who cherishes a fond and secret hope of seeing his brilliant boy following in his own footsteps. But the son knows better than the sire. At school and at college he has swept everything before him. His teachers have stood astonished at the ease and splendor of his triumphs. In every classical contest, Adoniram Judson was first and his rivals nowhere. His phenomenal success has awakened within him a proud and all-absorbing self-consciousness. The conquest that his dazzling intellectual endowments must win for him in the golden future fire his fancy with excited dreams. 'Day and night,' as one of his biographers puts it, 'he feels his ambition with visions of eminence and glory such as no mortal has yet won.

Now he is a second Homer, thrilling a nation with heroic lays; now a mighty statesman, guiding, with steady hand, the destinies of his country; but, whatever the dream of the moment, its nucleus is ever his own transcendent greatness.' A minister! *He* a Congregational minister! He smiles disdainfully at his father's lack of imagination.

This was in 1803; and in 1803 the hectic and amazing vogue of Tom Paine was at its very height. In every seat of learning it was considered the correct thing to pooh-pooh Christianity. It is said that at Yale every student was an avowed infidel. The graduates even adopted the names of the great French and English atheists, and asked to be addressed by those names in preference to their own. The imperious mind of Judson was swiftly infected by the prevailing epidemic. At Providence College, in the class above his own, was a young fellow named E——, a youth of rare genius, of sparkling wit, of high culture, and of charming personality. This senior student was powerfully attracted to Judson, and Judson was flattered and fascinated by his friendship. E—— was, however, one of the leaders of the new philosophy; and, in accepting his companionship and confidence, Judson committed himself irretrievably to an attitude of audacious and aggressive unbelief. In those days his father's dreams of ordination seemed to rest upon a singularly flimsy foundation.

II

But, as is so often the case, it was the unexpected
that happened. Wherever Adoniram Judson went,
in the course of his historic and adventurous career,
he carried with him, as Dr. Angus says, that evidence of the truth of Christianity which is at once
the most portable and the most conclusive—the vivid
memory of a startling and sensational conversion.

Our sceptical young student makes up his mind to
set out on horseback on a tour of the northern States.
He rests one night at a certain wayside inn.   The
landlord explains apologetically that the only room
that he can offer is one that adjoins an apartment in
which a young man is lying very ill—dying perhaps.
Judson assures the innkeeper that it does not matter;
death, he declares, is nothing to him; and, except
that he will feel a natural sympathy for the unfortunate sufferer, the circumstances will in no way dis-
turb him.

The partition between the two rooms is, however,
terribly thin.   In the stillness of the night, Judson
lies awake, listening to the groans of the dying man
—groans of anguish; groans, he sometimes fancies,
of despair.   The heartrending sounds powerfully
affect him.   But he pulls himself together.   What
would his college companions say if *they* knew of
his weakness?   And, above all, what would the clear-
minded, highly intellectual, sparklingly witty E——
say?   How, after feeling as he had felt, could he

look into the face of E—— again? But it is of no use. The awful sounds in the next room continue, and although he hides his head beneath the blankets, he hears everything—and shudders! At length, however, all is still. He rises at dawn; seeks the innkeeper; and inquires about his neighbor.

'He's dead!' is the blunt reply.

'Dead!' replies Judson. 'And who was he?'

'Oh,' explains the innkeeper languidly, 'he was a student from Providence College; a very fine fellow; his name was E——!'

Judson is completely stunned. He feels that he cannot continue his tour. He turns his horse's head towards his old home; opens his stricken heart to his father and mother; and begs them to help him to a faith that will stand the test of life and of death, of time and of eternity. Full of the thoughts that his parents suggest to him, he retires to the calm seclusion of Andover, and there, with nothing to distract his attention from the stupendous themes that are pressing upon his mind, he makes a solemn dedication of himself to God. He feels, beyond the shadow of a doubt, that he has become a new creature in Christ Jesus. Returning home, he gladdens everybody by announcing his momentous decision; and, in the year that marks his coming-of-age, he becomes a member of his father's Church.

During these memorable days of crisis and of consecration one overwhelming thought has taken pos-

session of his mind. *The love of Christ!* The love
that, in the days of his overweening pride and
selfish ambition, had not cast him off; the love that
had neither been estranged by his waywardness nor
alienated by his blatant and audacious unbelief; the
love that had followed him everywhere; the love that
would not let him go! Here, on my desk, are three
separate accounts of his conversion. In summing up
the situation, each writer refers to this factor in the
case.

'*The love of Christ* displaced selfish ambition as
the ruling motive of his life,' says the First.

'He became a man of one idea—*the love of Christ*
—and he desired to spend his whole life in demon-
strating it,' says the Second.

'Having been forgiven much, *he loved much,*' says
the Third.

*To comprehend the breadth and length and depth
and height and to know the love of Christ which
passeth knowledge*—this became, at the dawn of his
manhood, his one supreme and passionate aspiration.
It is the climax of all that has gone before; it is the
key of all that follows.

III

The depth and height of the love of Christ—he
knew something of the *depths* from which it could
rescue and of the *heights* to which it could raise.

But *the breadth and length of the love of Christ*—here was a new conception! The *breadth* and *length!* It seemed to embrace the whole wide world! And yet the world knew nothing of it! The idea took such a hold upon his mind that he could think of nothing else. He was haunted by the visions of nations dying in the dark. He started in his sleep at the thought of India, of Africa, and of China. The situation so appalled him that he became incapable of study. Then, one never-to-be-forgotten day, as he was taking a solitary walk in the woods, it seemed to him that the Saviour Himself drew near and said: *'Go ye into all the world and preach the gospel to every creature.'* His course was clear! Come wind, come weather, he must go!

But how? There was no Mission Board or Missionary Society to which he could apply. He talked it over with his fellow students until half a dozen of them were as eager as himself for such service. They petitioned the heads of the denomination, who, in their perplexity, laid the matter before the Churches. To the surprise of everybody, money poured in, and the newly formed committee was able to equip the mission-party, advancing each man a whole year's salary. Before leaving his native land, Judson had married. He and his bride sailed from Salem on February 18, 1812; they were welcomed at Calcutta by William Carey four months later; and, after a brief stay, set out for Burma. They reached Rangoon in July, 1813. Their first home was a rude hut built on a swamp outside the city wall. Wild beasts prowled around it. Near by, to the left, was the pit into which the offal of the city was poured. Near by, to the right, was the place where the bodies of the dead were buried. The young couple were sickened and disgusted by every sight and smell. On the day of their arrival, poor Mrs. Judson was too ill to walk or ride; she had to be carried to her unalluring home. Yet there was no repining. Both husband and wife smiled at the primitive conditions under which their first home was established; and, with brave hearts, they solemnly engaged to spend their entire lives among their barbarous and inhospitable neighbors.

IV

And they kept their word, although the price they had to pay was terrible beyond words. On one occasion we see Mr. Judson, starved to a skeleton, being driven in chains across the burning desert, until, his back bleeding beneath the lash and his feet blistered by the hot sand, he sinks, utterly exhausted, to the ground and prays for the merciful relief of a speedy death. On another occasion he is imprisoned for nearly two years in a foul and noisome den, his confinement being embittered by every device that a barbarous and malignant brutality could invent. He must have sunk under the fierce ordeal had not Mrs. Judson, often under cover of darkness, crept to the door of his horrid cell and ministered to him. For three weeks, it is true, she absented herself from the prison; but, when she returned, she bore a little child in her arms to explain her delinquency. Shortly afterwards the mission-house was stripped of every comfort; Mrs. Judson is left without even a chair or seat of any kind. To add to her troubles, Mary, her elder child, develops small-pox. Under the terrific strain, the poor mother finds herself unable to nurse her baby, and its pitiful cries intensify her anguish. In sheer desperation, she bribes the jailers to release her husband for an hour or two. And, whilst *she* applies herself to the little patient who is tossing in the delirium of the dreaded scourge, *he* carries the baby into the village, begging the nursing-mothers there to pity and to nourish it.

The crisis passed; but passed to be followed by others. It was announced that Mr. Judson's imprisonment was to be terminated by his execution. The exact date and hour were proclaimed; and husband and wife braced themselves for the tragic separation. In the interval, however, he was smuggled away, and the distracted wife had no inkling as to what had become of him. And one of the most pitiful and pathetic pages in the annals of Christian missions is the page that describes the subsequent return of Mr. Judson to his stricken home. *He* was

scarred, maimed, and emaciated by long suffering;
she was so worn and haggard that he could scarcely
recognize her.   Her glossy black curls had all been
shaved from her finely shaped head.   She was
dressed in rags—the only garments left her—and
everything about her told of extreme wretchedness
and privation.

And, before he had been fourteen years in Burma,
he had buried his wife and all his children there.
Yet, through it all, he never for a moment doubted
the reality and richness of *the love of Christ*.

'The love of Christ!' he says again and again, in
his letters, 'the breadth and length and depth and
height of the love of Christ!   If I had not felt certain that every additional trial was ordered by
infinite love and mercy, I could not have survived
my accumulated sufferings.'

V

But there were joys as well as sorrows.   That
was a great and golden day on which, after six long
years of diligent labor, he welcomed his first convert.   He never forgot the emotions with which,
that day, he and Mrs. Judson took the Communion
with a son of the soil who had entered into a deep
and transforming realization of the wonder of the
love of Christ.

On that day he set before himself two lofty aims.

He prayed that he might live to translate the entire Bible into the native language, and to preside over a native Church of at least one hundred members. He more than realized both ambitions. He not only translated the whole Bible into the Burman tongue, but wrote, in addition, many valuable pamphlets in the native language. And, before he had been twenty years in Burma, he had baptized his hundredth convert. After more than thirty years he revisited his native land.

'Behold,' exclaimed the chairman of the great meeting that welcomed him at Richmond, Virginia, 'behold what a change God hath wrought in Burma! The entire Bible has been skilfully translated, carefully revised, accurately printed, and eagerly read. In a land so recently enveloped in darkness and superstition, many vigorous Churches have been planted. Native preachers have been raised up to proclaim, in their own tongue, and among their own people, the unsearchable riches of Christ. The Karens, a simple-hearted and singular people, are turning by hundreds and thousands to the Lord. Among them the gospel has met with a success rarely equalled since the days of the apostles. On Burma the morning light is breaking!'

And, in achieving these notable triumphs, Mr. Judson adhered constantly to his old theme. 'Think much on *the love of Christ!*' he used to say to all his converts and inquirers, 'think much on *the love of*

Christ!' He seemed convinced, as Dr. Wayland
says, that the whole world could be converted if only
each separate individual could be persuaded that
there was a place for him in the divine love.

VI

'Think much on *the love of Christ!'* It was the
keynote of all his days. He returned to his beloved
Burma; but he was never quite the same again. His
health was shattered and his strength was spent. It
was clear that his time was short. But in one respect,
at least, he was unchanged. He talked with even
greater fervor, frequency, and fondness of the
deathless love of his Lord. 'And,' adds his biographer, 'if he found anything clouding his consciousness and enjoyment of *the love of Christ,* he
would go away into the jungle and live there by himself until the sweetness of his faith had been restored
to him.'

He died at sea. In the course of that last voyage,
undertaken in search of health, he harped continually
on the one familiar string. Mr. Thomas Ranney,
who accompanied him, says that he kept repeating
one text: *'As I have loved you, so ought ye to love
one another.'* *'As I have loved you,'* he would
exclaim; *'as I have loved you!'* and then he would
cry ecstatically: 'Oh, the love of Christ! *The love
of Christ!'*

Later, when confined to his berth, he would talk of nothing else. 'Oh, the love of Christ! *The love of Christ!*' he would murmur, his eye kindling with enthusiasm and the tears chasing each other down his cheeks. *'The love of Christ—its breadth and length and depth and height*—we cannot comprehend it now—but what a study for eternity!' And, even after he had lost the power of speech, his lips still framed in silence the familiar syllables *'The love of Christ! The love of Christ!'*

A few days before he passed, he spoke, with evident pleasure, of being buried at sea. It gave, he said, a sense of freedom and expansion; it contrasted agreeably with the dark and narrow grave to which he had committed so many whom he loved. The vast blue ocean, into which his body was lowered a day or two later, seemed to his dying fancy a symbol of his Saviour's unfathomable and boundless love—the love that passeth knowledge—the love that knows neither measure nor end, neither sounding nor shore.

12

JUDE BIRT'S TEXT

Character in *The Backsliders* by William Lindsay.

2 Corinthians 4:7

I

'EVERY one will turn and look at me and smile,' said Jude Birt, when the Rev. John Gray expressed his intention of preaching on that particular text. 'Every one will turn and smile, for I've about wore them words threadbare!'

The minister assured him that the words would never wear out; although, had he been pressed, he would have been forced to admit that the text had at times sustained considerable damage as a result of the violent treatment to which Jude had subjected it.

The episode occurs towards the end of *The Backsliders,* but the three characters that I have mentioned—Jude Birt, John Gray, and the text—meet very frequently in Mr. William Lindsay's delightful pages. They meet, for example, in the very first chapter.

John Gray—tall, straight, clean-shaven, a dignified and good-looking young man of twenty-five, clad in clerical black—is the new minister at Wesley, and has just arrived by train. He looks up and down the platform to see if any one has come to welcome him; but nobody has. He is inquiring of the stationmaster concerning the movements of the coach, when his bag is suddenly seized, and his hand grasped, by as odd a specimen of humanity as he could have hoped to see. The new-comer is of medium height, round-shouldered and freckle-faced, with open brow and deep-set blue eyes. His clothes are badly faded and hang loosely upon him; he wears a winter cap with ear-flaps, and carries a whip in his hand.

'You come right along with me,' he exclaims. 'I'm Jude Birt, the stage-driver, an' I s'pose you're the new preacher. I'm awful glad to see yer!'

On the road they discussed many things, and at length came in sight of their destination.

'There's the spire of Wesley Church right ahead,' exclaimed Jude. 'The only thing ag'in it is that I'm a member; but you mustn't take me for a sample.' Jude was honestly sorry that the minister's first impression of his new flock had to be based upon so unfortunate a representative. 'But of course,' he went on, 'the Bible says: *"We have this treasure in earthen vessels."* It's my favorite text, an' I git considerable consolation outer it.'

'It's a good text,' replied the minister, 'but we must not take it as an excuse for our shortcomings.'

And so our trio—the stage-driver, the minister,

and the text—meet for the first time; and in that
introductory meeting the minister puts his finger on
the weak spots in poor Jude's theology. It was at
his first meeting with his new office-bearers that
John Gray saw the significance of his own remark.
At that meeting David French, the secretary, was
unusually excited. Even before the meeting began
he paced the room restlessly. David was an
extremely capable fellow, the youngest member of
the Board, and it was understood that he intended
entering the ministry.

'What makes you so uneasy, David?' asked Belcher, one of the other officers.

'It's an awful thing,' replied David, 'to turn any
one out of the church. It's like excommunication; I
want no part in it.'

'Oh, you'll get used to it,' said Belcher; 'it's harder
on Mr. Harding, with Faith, his own daughter, coming before us. How many are there?'

'Fred Miller for wordliness, Abbey Green for
slander, Jude Birt for drunkenness, and Faith Harding for——' David would neither mention nor listen
to the accusation against Faith; Faith had a name-
less baby in her arms. But we are only concerned
with Jude.

'Jude Birt for drunkenness.'

'It's my favorite text,' said Jude: ' *"We have this
treasure in earthen vessels";* I get considerable consolation outer it.'

'A good text,' replied the minister, drawing a bow at a venture, 'but we must not take it as an excuse for our shortcomings.'

John Gray preached many powerful sermons at Wesley in the days that followed; but he never preached a more timely or more pointed sermon than that.

II

'We have this treasure in earthen vessels.' That was *Jude Birt's Text;* and those who have read the story know how frequently he quoted it. It is well worth quoting. The Treasure and the Vessel! The Heavenly Treasure and the Earthen Vessel! The Heavenly Treasure is the Divine Light; the Earthen Vessel is the Human Lamp that holds it. Paul is saying that he lives, not to preach himself—the lamp, the Earthen Vessel—but to preach Christ—the Light of the Ages, the Heavenly Treasure. And he goes on to say that *'God, who commanded the light to shine out of darkness, hath shined in our hearts to give the light of the knowledge of the glory of God in the face of Jesus Christ. But,'* he adds, *'we have this treasure in earthen vessels, that the excellency of the power may be of God and not of us.'* Matthew Henry, Fawcett, and other teachers think that Paul is referring to the earthen pitchers that held the lights with which Gideon and his Ironsides confounded and

destroyed the Midianites. However that may be, his meaning is unmistakable. Dr. Denney says that 'the earthen vessel which holds the priceless treasure of the knowledge of God—the lamp of frail ware in which the light of Christ's glory shines for the illumination of the world—is human nature as it is; man's body in its weakness and liability to death; his mind with its limitations and confusions; his moral nature with its distortions and misconceptions.' *This* is the earthen vessel. 'And,' says Chrysostom, 'it is one of the most marvellous proofs of God's power, that an earthen vessel can bear such splendor and hold such a treasure!'

And what then? Shall I be careless of the earthen pitcher because it is only an earthen pitcher? Shall I allow it to become damaged and defiled? That was Jude Birt's mistake. Jude forgot that, when the earthen lamp is cracked and contaminated, it can no longer act as a medium for the heavenly light. And not only so. The lamp that can hold no light is a mockery and a vexation. The officers at Wesley were right in asking themselves whether such a deceptive and discreditable vessel ought not to be thrown to the rubbish-heap. Why should Jude's name be permitted to remain upon the roll? 'There are earthen vessels which are yet clean,' says Bengel, 'and there are golden vessels which are filthy.' But what if the *earthen* vessel becomes filthy? That was the question which Jude had ignored; it was the question that the officers at Wesley were forced to consider. The lamp may be very common and very fragile; yet, if clean, it may illumine the darkest and dreariest path on earth. But, if defiled, it is useless, and worse than useless. Jude had no right to make the earthenware composition of the lamp an excuse for the noisome smoke that it gave forth in place of light. *'We have this treasure in earthen vessels.'* 'That is my favorite text,' he said; but his partiality for the passage was based on the mischievous interpretation that he placed upon it.

III

Mr. Lindsay's charming story has to do with a number of very doubtful saints whose hearts were eventually sweetened, whose characters were ennobled, and whose lives were transformed, through discovering the real significance of *Jude Birt's Text.* There are two sets of people in the book—the backsliders and their judges. Those who judged the backsliders were really very excellent people; but their virtues were disfigured by a smug self-satisfaction, an overwhelming consciousness of their spiritual superiority, and a cold severity towards smudged souls like Jude and Faith. As the story develops, these chaste but chilling spirits come to see that the lustre of which they are so proud is the lustre, not of the *lamp,* but of the *light.* The lamp is of the earth, earthy. Each discovers in himself frailties that he had never before suspected. The treasure that he holds is extremely precious; but it is deposited in a vessel that is of the commonest possible clay. Such discoveries make good men wonderfully sympathetic and wonderfully tolerant.

Then, of course, there were the backsliders. Some of them, like Jude Birt, had sinned openly. Others, like David French, the secretary—whose compassion for his dying mother alone prevented him from publicly acknowledging his complicity in poor Faith's shame—had sinned terribly but secretly. And, in each case, three distinct processes operated simultaneously.

(*a*) Each discovered to his humiliation and dismay the treachery of his own heart; he saw that the divine light had been committed to a vessel made out of the soil.

(*b*) Each, softened and made sensitive by the consciousness of his pitiful infirmity, looked with eyes of tender compassion upon others whose besetments, though different in form, were similar in character to his own.

(*c*) Each, finding himself treated with intelligent and affectionate sympathy by those who, at last, really seemed to understand him, responded to the genial spring-time atmosphere that such generous behavior wove about him, and brought forth fruits meet for repentance. Truly loved, each became truly lovely. *Jude Birt's Text* became everybody's text. Three of the Church officers were discussing Jude one night—the passage occurs in the early part of the book.

'Every Saturday night, after eight, Jude is in no condition to tell the time by looking at the clock,' said Belcher.

'He's not fit to be a Church member. If we can't clear the Church of such backsliders, how can we expect the showers of blessing promised in the Bible?' asked Harding.

'It's all right to be down on sin,' replied David French, 'but we mustn't be too hard on the sinner. *"We have this treasure in earthen vessels,"* the Good Book says.'

'You're right, Dave,' exclaimed Belcher. 'That's *Jude's favorite text*. We're all *earthen vessels;* the Good Book says the best of us make mistakes. That's the reason they put rubbers on lead pencils.'

Here, mark you, is David French, the Church secretary, quoting the text in reference to Jude. And, twenty pages farther on, I find Jude, no longer sheltering himself behind the text, quoting it in reference to David.

'There's lots worse fellers than Dave French,' asserted Jude, 'an' we're all *earthen vessels,* the best of us.'

It was a glorious Sunday, the Sunday on which Faith and Jude made public confession of their

backslidings. 'As John Gray walked up the hill to
the Church, it seemed as if the whole world had made
confession and had been cleansed and purified. The
sky was swept clear of every cloud, and the sun sent
down its benediction.' The minister's heart was
very tender that morning. 'He read the fourth chapter of Second Corinthians, and Jude smiled up at him
when he came to the verse which the stage-driver
loved: *"But we have this treasure in earthen vessels,
that the excellency of the power may be of God and
not of us."'* John preached that morning on the
wonder of the divine forgiveness. 'Sin,' he said, 'is
not only forgiven, but forgotten, by God. It is as if
it had not been at all. We are cleansed from all un-
righteousness. The Church, therefore, should take
back the repentant sinner and forget his sin. The
member of the Church who points a finger of scorn
at an erring brother or sister is guilty of a dreadful
wrong. Which of us can claim the right to cast the
first stone? *"We have this treasure in earthen
vessels."'*

IV

And so a new spirit saturated the little community.
Each member, remembering his own frailty, treated
the others with sympathy and charity. And the most
astonishing results quickly followed. Jude forsook
his drunkenness for ever. Faith made her brave and

beautiful confession. David French took his place by her side and made her his wedded wife. Mr. Harding—previously so cold and proud—welcomed his erring daughter to his heart and home once more. Surprised and delighted at such transformations, the members soon acquired the habit of treating the men and women of the town with similar compassion. Pasco Tripp was the worst man in the neighborhood.

'Poor Pasc ain't got the grace of God in his heart,' said Jude, 'but the Good Book says: *"We have this treasure in earthen vessels"*—just *earthen vessels*. That means that the best of us ain't got no occasion to feel puffed up. I know I'm half-baked clay, an' cracked at that; and, sure, I ain't got nothing to say agin Pasc.'

And, to such treatment, those *outside* responded, as those *within* had done. Even Alice Hale, the beautiful and cultured sceptic, capitulated. She was an artist—had she not painted an exquisite picture of Faith and her baby as the Madonna and Child?—and her artist eye saw something unspeakably beautiful in the new atmosphere at Wesley.

'When you first came to Wesley,' she told the minister, 'I was a pagan. I worshipped beauty only. I had little faith in God; less in man's goodness; still less in what is called religion; least of all in the Church. You've half converted me!' Her conversion was soon complete, and so was many another.

And, although Mr. Lindsay does not say so, the

beauty of it all must have been that, knowing the earlier frailties of Jude and David, and the other members of the little Church, the townspeople can have had no difficulty in recognizing that the radiance that streamed from Wesley Church was the radiance, not of the earthen lamps, but of the light divine. *'We have this treasure in earthen vessels, that the excellency of the power may be of God and not of us.'* 'The light of life,' says President Hugh Jones, D.D., of Llangollen College, 'the light of life was deposited in *earthen* vessels belonging to the terrestrial world, and not in the *golden* vessels of the celestial city. Had it been placed in the shining vessels of the city of God, many of the spectators would have ascribed the brilliancy of the light to the shining quality of the *vessels* and not to the supernatural brightness of the divine *light* itself. But God ordained that the vessels should be made of clay, that the glory might be ascribed to the light and not to the vessels in which it is deposited.'

If Samson had smitten the Philistines with some glittering Excalibur, we should have fixed our attention on the splendid sword; as it is, we look contemptuously on the jawbone in his hand and magnify the might of his strong right arm. When the musician delights us with the strains that he draws from his beloved Cremona, we are apt to think wonderingly of the violin; but when some Paganini wooes the most bewitching harmonies from an old fiddle with a broken string, we lose ourselves in admiration of the master. Therein lies the real significance of *Jude Birt's Text*. For when the men of this world see the light of the knowledge of the glory of God streaming from lives that they know to be of the most human texture, they look up in astonishment, and adore the grace that can transmute pitchers of clay into lamps of such lustre that they flood the ways of earth with the very light of heaven.

13

GENERAL C. G. GORDON'S TEXT

1833–1885
British colonial officer and administrator.

1 John 4:15

I

GORDON, as The Times finely said, is one of Plutarch's men. He ranks with the heroes of antiquity, with the warriors of renown, with the knights of romance, the men who never die. A hero of heroes, Mr. Gladstone calls him. 'He was,' says Lord Morley, 'a soldier of infinite personal courage and daring; of striking military energy, initiative, and resource; a high, pure, and single character dwelling much in the region of the unseen.' His photograph is imprinted upon all our minds. We seem strangely familiar with his short and unimpressive stature; with his fine head, that always seemed a size too large for him; with his well-moulded face, lively and rich in eloquent expressiveness; with the short, curly hair that had once been raven black; and, above all, with his clear blue eye, full of merriment, yet capable of startling gravity—the eye that seemed to look you through and through. He was never created a knight or called to the peerage; yet his contemporaries smothered him with popular titles that expressed the honor and affection in which everybody held him.

They called him the Swordless Conqueror, the Ever-Victorious General, the Uncrowned King. 'With celestial vigor armed, and plain heroic magnitude of mind,' he lived his glorious life, and wove about his name a lustre that can never fade. 'History,' as Lord Cromer justly observes, 'history has recorded few incidents more calculated to stir the imagination than that presented by this brave man, who, strong in the faith which sustained him, stood undismayed amidst dangers which might well have appalled the stoutest heart.' Nobody can saunter along the stately aisles of St. Paul's without being touched by the simple yet exquisite tribute that adorns the Gordon monument. *'At all times and everywhere,'* it affirms, *'he gave his strength to the weak, his substance to the poor, his sympathy to the suffering, and his heart to God.'* Was ever so pacific a record inscribed on the memorial of an illustrious soldier?

II

He gave his heart to God, says that inscription. There lies the secret! It is natural that the ponderous biographies of Gordon—and their name is Legion—should deal primarily, almost exclusively, with the military exploits and administrative triumphs that won for him an honorable and deathless renown. The distinguished services that he rendered to the Empire in China, in Egypt, and in the Sudan will never be forgotten by a grateful nation. Yet, as his innumerable biographers confess, the grandeur of his record is based on the sublimity of his character; and the sublimity of his character is based on the simplicity of his faith. His faith is quite easily the biggest thing about him. 'No soldier,' says Lord Cromer, in augmenting the tribute that I have already quoted, 'no soldier about to lead a forlorn hope, no Christian martyr tied to the stake or thrown to the wild beasts of ancient Rome, ever faced death with more unconcern than General Gordon. His faith was sublime. Strong in that faith, he could meet the savage who plunged a spear into his breast with a gesture of scorn, and with the sure and certain hope of immortality which has been promised by the Master in whose footsteps he endeavored to tread.'

That robust but simple faith took possession of his heart whilst he was yet in his teens. Originally intended for the Artillery, he was sent to the Academy at Woolwich. But here his high and untamed spirit proved his undoing. In the course of one escapade he threw an officer downstairs; in the course of another he hit a recruit over the head with a clothes-brush. Determined to suppress such horseplay, the authorities told the young madcap that they must withhold his commission for six months. In disgust, Gordon turned his back on the Artillery and sought refuge with the Royal Engineers. The change involved his transfer from the Academy at Woolwich to the forts at Pembroke. And, at Pembroke, Gordon came face to face with destiny.

For at Pembroke the impetuous youth fell under the influence of a certain Captain Drew. Drew was a particularly attractive fellow, but he had one amazing foible. He insisted on talking to Gordon in quiet moments about the grace of God, about the redeeming love of Christ, and about the forgiveness of sins! He even took from his pocket a New Testament and directed Gordon's attention to the great evangelistic promises! 'Why,' exclaimed Gordon, in astonishment, 'you *talk* just as my sister *writes*. In every letter Augusta begs me to turn to the Saviour!' Between two fires, he soon surrendered. He tells his sister of the joy with which he has yielded his life to Christ. The Bible is a new book to him; and in every other respect his tastes have radically changed. He finds special pleasure in reading *The Remains of Murray McCheyne* and Scott's *Commentaries*. 'No novels,' he tells his sister, 'can compare with the *Commentaries* of Scott. I well remember when you used to get them in monthly parts and I used to laugh at them; but, thank God, it is different with me now. I feel much happier and more contented than I used to do.' In the rough and tumble of the Crimean War, in which he is commended for conspicuous gallantry, and in his

earliest experiences in China, his faith becomes
slightly obscured. But an attack of small-pox at
Tientsin recalls him to his better self. 'I am glad to
say,' he tells Augusta, 'that this disease has brought
me back to my Saviour, and I trust in future to be
a better Christian than I have been hitherto.' From
that hour he never looked back. He preserved the
simplicity of his faith to the end.

III

Gordon never married. He formed no close ties
or intimate friendships. How could he? The rov-
ing nature of his commissions sentenced him to
solitude. He lived a lonely life and died a lonely
death. But he cherished one sublime companionship. His Bible and he were inseparable. He was
a man of one book, as Mr. Lytton Strachey points
out, but he read and re-read that book with an untir-
ing and unending assiduity. 'In all his Odysseys,
in all his strange and agitated adventures, a day
never passed on which he neglected the voice of
eternal wisdom as it spoke through the words of
Paul or Solomon, of Jonah or Habakkuk. The
doubts of philosophers, the investigations of com-
mentators, the smiles of men of the world, the dog-
mas of Churches—these meant nothing to him. Two
facts alone were evident; there was the Bible and
there was himself; and all that remained to be done

was for him to discover what were the Bible's instructions, and to act accordingly. That being so, it was only necessary for him to read the Bible over and over and over again; and, therefore, for the rest of his life he did so.' When Lord Cromer wrote to Gordon urging him to take some startling step that would precipitate a decisive issue, Gordon replied that he would consult the prophet Isaiah about it.

Few people felt the tragic death of Gordon more than Queen Victoria. Her Majesty's letters to Miss Gordon throb with passionate emotion and profoundest sympathy. In response, Miss Gordon presented the Queen with her brother's Bible; and it is still one of the most honored treasures preserved at Windsor Castle.

In March, 1885 [says the Archbishop of Canterbury], I was brought into vital touch with the springs of that extraordinary life of adventure and leadership which had closed in dark tragedy two months before. For I was entrusted with the interesting task of examining the little Bible which had been for so many long and dusty years General Gordon's daily companion and guide, and which has now an honored resting-place in the corridor in Windsor Castle. It would not be easy to describe that little book—worn and thumbed from cover to cover and scored and annotated with different colored inks and pencils in pursuance of separate lines of thought. But one trait throughout its pages he that runs might read. It is the thought of the man's steady, unswerving confidence in the daily guidance of his God, finding that guidance after his own fashion in proverbs and story, in psalm and prophecy, in gospel and vision. That little book, carefully mended with fine whip-cord by his own hand, had been 'his all-sufficient

solace and unerring guide on Chinese marches, in Danubian
fields, amidst the solitudes of the African desert, and in the
camps of the slave-traders.

When Gordon left England for the last time he
presented every member of the British Cabinet with
a copy of Dr. Samuel Clarke's *Scripture Promises.*
He would fain infect the mightiest in the land with
his own unwavering confidence in the Scriptures.

IV

But, in that well-worn Bible of his, there is one
passage to which he turned more fondly and more
frequently than to any other.   He regarded that
golden sentence as the key to the entire volume.   In
his correspondence he quotes it again and again.
*'Whosoever shall confess that Jesus is the Son of
God, God dwelleth in him, and he in God.'*
    'The indwelling of God!' he writes.   'The Bible
is a sealed book until you realize this truth.   It is
sure and certain; God lives and works in those who
fearlessly confess His Son.'
    And again, in a leaflet which he had printed both
in English and French, he says: 'You really believe
in your heart that Jesus is the Son of God?   Then
God dwells within you! *For "whosoever shall confess that Jesus is the Son of God, God dwelleth in
him, and he in God."* And if you say to Him: O
Lord, I believe that Jesus is the Son of God; show

me, for His sake, that Thou livest in me, He will make you *feel* His presence in your heart.'

And once more, in his *Reflections in Palestine,* he says: "My comfort is that, if we believe in Jesus, He dwells in us, and we become members of His body. This is my prayer—the prayer that the simplest of us can make—"O Lord, who dost live in all who believe that Jesus is Thy Son, make me to feel Thy presence more and more!"'

The believing heart!
The witnessing lips!
The indwelling God!

'Whosoever shall confess that Jesus is the Son of God, God dwelleth in him, and he in God.'

Here, in a word, is the essence of the faith to which our martial-mystic, our soldier-saint, so implicitly and persistently clung.

V

'Whosoever shall confess that Jesus is the Son of God, God dwelleth in him, and he in God.'

By far the best exposition of General Gordon's text is Martin Luther's. 'If,' says Luther, 'if you had knocked at the door of my heart any time *before my conversion* and had asked, Who dwells in here? I would have answered that no one dwells here but Martin Luther! And if I had opened the door, and you had come in, you would have seen a raw-headed monk, with a shaven crown and a hair shirt, with two tables of stone under his pillow and a knotted scourge hanging beside his bed. But if you were to knock at the door of my heart *to-night,* I would answer that Martin Luther no longer lives here; Jesus Christ alone lives here!' So it was with Gordon. At Pembroke, as he listened to the voice of Captain Drew and read the letters of his sister, he seemed to hear the Saviour of the World knocking, ever knocking, at the portals of his soul. *'Behold, I stand at the door and knock: if any man hear My voice, and open the door, I will come in to him.'*

'I will come in to him!' Gordon opened the door, welcomed the divine Guest, and experienced that wondrous indwelling for the rest of his days. Throughout his illustrious but lonely life that *Inner Presence* meant everything to him. By its mystic virtue he slew everything base that lurked within his soul. A man of like passions with ourselves, he was subject to severe besetments. For one thing, he was plagued with a particularly explosive temper; and, for another, he discovered, during one stage of his career, the insidious fascination of alcohol. Mr. Strachey shows how, under a fierce tropical sun, his Bible found an ugly rival in his flask. The fiery liquors inflamed the fiery temper; the outbursts of passion were followed by fits of moodiness and depression, in the course of which Gordon again sought solace in the bottle; and so the two evils acted

and reacted upon each other. Fortified by the *Inner Presence,* however, he eventually trod these temptations underfoot and tasted the joy that only conquerors know.

Still impelled by that *Inner Presence,* Gordon spent the little time he had in England in reading his Bible to the aged poor, and in imparting its sacred truths to the ragged boys that he gathered around him. Prompted by the monitions of that *Inner Presence,* he poured out his money as if it had been water. He gave away all that he had, and sometimes more than all. 'The silver tea-set at home,' he used to say, 'can be sold to pay my funeral expenses!' His funeral expenses! The tragedy was that, in his case, there were none!

Strong in the sense of that *Divine Indwelling,* he knew no fear—even at the last. The Mahdi sent him an Eastern costume. 'Put it on,' he said, 'as a sign that you renounce your faith, and no harm shall come to you!' Gordon flung the clothes to the ground and trampled upon them in the sight of everybody. 'Then, alone, he went up to the roof of his high palace and turned the telescope, almost mechanically, to the north.' He looked—but looked in vain—for the relieving columns that never arrived. 'I am quite happy,' he says, in his last letter to his sister, 'I am quite happy, thank God, and, like Lawrence, I have tried to do my duty!' A few hours later his head was fixed on a tree beside the public highway, and every passer-by threw stones at it. But what did that matter to him? With heroic fortitude he had presented his breast to the spears of his enemies; and his journals show that the *Abiding Guest* was with him to the end.

14

CHARLES KINGSLEY'S TEXT

1819–1875

English clergyman and novelist.

1 John 4:8, 15

I

CHARLES KINGSLEY made up his mind that, if he could not make history in one way, he would in another. Novelist, poet, economist, reformer, preacher, philosopher, historian, professor, he touched the soul of England at an infinite number of points. His intense and passionate spirit welcomed any avenue by which he might give expression to the thoughts that surged so furiously within him. His message burned within his bones, and he was glad to utter it anywhere, anyhow. His critics pillory this intensity of his; it is, they say, his worst fault. 'Kingsley never speaks,' Stopford Brooke complains; 'he screams! If he tells you that it is five o'clock, he says it in such a way that you imagine that it is the crack of doom.' J. R. Green, the historian, passes a similar censure. 'After dinner,' he says, 'Kingsley paced up and down the room like a caged tiger, uttering his convictions on all sorts of subjects with extraordinary excitement and animation.'

To see Kingsley at his best, however, we must see him in the dreamy old rectory at Eversley, the

secluded Hampshire village in which most of his
life was spent. Let us peep in upon him there! He
is a tall, spare man, thin as a lath, and sinewy rather
than powerful. His face, marked by rare delicacy
and intelligence, is as keen as a sword. He is of
swarthy complexion, dark hair, and bright, piercing,
deep-set eyes. In spite of his nervous, excitable temperament, he is of a gentle and affectionate disposition. The soul of chivalry, his hot temper, usually
under rigid control, reveals itself in a flashing scorn
and a fiery indignation whenever anything ignoble
or impure presents itself to him. His study opens
on to the lawn, and the lawn has become a necessary
adjunct to the study. For his excitement, as he
bends over his manuscript, often becomes so intense
that, in order to calm himself, he snatches up his
long clay pipe and strides out on to the grass. Having paced to and fro for a while, his fine features
twitching with ungovernable emotion, he at length
feels that he can trust himself, with some approxi-
mation to judicial calm, to resume the thread of his
story. His critics would say that the green lawn and
the clay pipe occasionally scamped their soothing
work. They allowed their effervescent master to
return to his desk before his agitation had completely subsided. In his *Victorian Age in Literature,*
Mr. Chesterton says that *Westward Ho!* is a lie;
but he hastens to add that it is a good, thundering,
honest lie. Nothing worse could be said of Kings-

ley—and nothing better. He himself would have appreciated both the criticism and the compliment.

II

The gates of the Kingdom of Heaven swung open to Charles Kingsley on the day on which he fell in love. It is impossible to disentangle his love-story from the history of his spiritual pilgrimage. I dreamed the other night that I had somehow fallen into a controversial mood, and was fiercely assailing the doctrine of the celibacy of the clergy. If, in this world or any other, that dream comes true, I shall have a good deal to say about Charles Kingsley. For, if Charles Kingsley had never met Fanny Grenfell, he would certainly never have made history; would, indeed, have remained the veriest nonentity. Towards the end of his life, Kingsley was asked to mention the most notable date in his career. He replied unhesitatingly—July 6, 1839. It was the day on which he saw Mrs. Kingsley's face for the first time. 'That,' he used to say, 'was my *real* wedding-day.' It was more than that. For, in some subtle and mysterious way, it precipitated a profound spiritual crisis. It lifted him from the murky by-ways of doubt to the sunny uplands of a clear and intelligent faith. It led him out of the horror and tyranny of sin into the exuberant assurance and enjoyment of salvation.

On that never-to-be-forgotten day in July Kingsley felt that love was *delicious*. But he felt more; he felt that love was *divine*. Love, he said to himself, what is love? Love is—God! Or, to put it the other way round, *God is love!* The New Testament says as much: '*God is love, and he that dwelleth in love dwelleth in God, and God in him.*' From that very hour, *this* was Kingsley's text—the text that summarized, in the simplest possible way, his radiant and remarkable experience; the text that epitomized the essence of his teaching; the text that reflected, as Mrs. Kingsley tells us, the essential spirit of his life.

When Charles Kingsley died in 1875, at the age of fifty-six, a resting-place in Westminster Abbey was immediately offered; but the family, knowing his wishes, decided that he should lie in the pretty little churchyard at Eversley, beside the villagers among whom all his days had been spent. A beautiful monument, surmounted by a bust by Woolner, has, however, been placed in one of the choicest nooks in the Abbey. Both the tomb in Hampshire and the memorial at Westminster are frequently visited. 'The green turf round his grave,' says Mrs. Kingsley, 'was soon worn by the tread of many footsteps; a day seldom passed without strangers being seen in the churchyard. On Bank Holidays, numbers would come to see his last resting-place. Little children, who had loved the *Water-babies* and the *Heroes,* would kneel down reverently to look at the beautiful wreaths which kind hands had placed there, while the gipsies never passed the gate without turning in to stand over the grave in silence.'

And he who passes from the white marble cross in that country churchyard to the chaste memorial in the stately Abbey will find one feature common to both. For, on both, a text has been inscribed—Kingsley's text: *'God is Love.'* It was, says Mrs. Kingsley, the keynote of his faith.

III

The story of Kingsley's wedded life is one of the sweetest idylls of English literature. That luxurious summer day in July, 1839, was Kingsley's golden day —the day when his star appeared to him as the star appeared to the Magi; the day on which the angels sang to him as the angels sang on the plains of Bethlehem; and, as of old, the star and the angels led to the Saviour. It was the day on which earth became vocal, luminous, celestial, divine! Three years later a friend called at his cottage at Eversley, where Kingsley was then curate. 'I found him,' says this casual caller, 'almost beside himself, stamping his goods and chattels into a portmanteau. "My dear fellow," I exclaimed, "what on earth is the matter?" "I am engaged!" he cried ecstatically, "I am engaged; and I am going to see her *now—to-day!*" I was delighted, and left him to his joy.'

They were married early in 1844. Never were two lives more perfectly blended. 'To his marriage,' says an intimate friend, 'Kingsley owed the whole tenor of his life, all that he possessed and enjoyed. For more than thirty years, his every word and look seemed to show the sense of boundless gratitude that had become part of his nature. Whenever he turned to Mrs. Kingsley, or referred to her, it was with a gesture of chivalrous devotion.' His wedded bliss was so perfect that he would not listen to any suggestion of its discontinuance in another life. He was twitted with the text that says that in heaven they neither marry nor are given in marriage. 'All that I can say about that text,' he replied, 'is that it has nothing to do with me and my wife. What I feel to her now, I shall feel for ever. I say deliberately that, if I do not love my wife, body and soul, as well *there* as I do *here,* then there is no real resurrection of my body, or of my soul, and *I* shall not be *I.'*

Towards the end of 1874, Mrs. Kingsley's health suddenly failed. As Christmas drew near, death seemed to be hovering over the little rectory. He was told by the doctors that the case was quite hopeless. 'With those words,' he exclaimed, 'my own death-warrant was signed.' In point of fact, he never recovered from the blow, and was the first to go. For a little while he was able to minister beside his wife's bed. *'God is love,'* he said, in the midst of his anguish; and he spoke much of the indestructibility of such a marriage-tie as theirs. Then he took to his bed, and the two would correspond with each other by means of pencil notes borne by the nurse from room to room. And then, believing that Mrs. Kingsley would die first, and that he would be left in desolate loneliness, he gathered up all his strength for a final act of devotion. 'The last flash of genius from his breaking heart was to gather into three simple pregnant words, as a last offering to her, the whole story of his life, of his faith, and of his marriage. He was spared the agony that he dreaded. *He* was taken and *she* was left. And, at the foot of that marble cross at Eversley, Mrs. Kingsley inscribed, as a tribute to *him,* the three words that, with his dying hand, he had prepared as a final homage to *her: 'Amavimus: amamus: amabimus'* ('We loved: we love: we shall love').

IV

But, beautiful as all this is, there is a deeper beauty underlying it. What was it that happened on that July day in 1839, when Kingsley came to feel that love was not only *delicious,* but *divine?*

In those days, I learn from his biography, his mind was agitated by a hurricane of doubt; and his face, with its unsatisfied, hungry, and even defiant look, bore painful witness to the state of his mind. It had, too, a sad, longing expression which seemed to indicate that he had all his life been looking for a sympathy he had never yet found, a rest which he could never hope to attain. His peculiar character had never been understood; his heart had been asleep. 'An athiest I never was,' he says, 'but in my early life I wandered through a labyrinth of doubt and made many vain attempts to explain to myself the insoluble riddle of life.' 'I have no spiritual guide,' he writes to a friend; 'I am told that before I can avail myself of the benevolence of Him in whom you trust I must believe in His Godhead and Omnipotence. I do not so believe. And, what is more, I cannot even pray.' There were times when he thought of giving up the maddening quest and forgetting all such abstract torments in the excitement of a wild life on the prairies of the Far West.

'His heart was asleep,' the biography says. But the time of awakening had come. It was like dawn after dark, like spring after winter. Love came into his life. The Word became Flesh. And, somehow, beneath the spell of that new influence, faith seemed wonderfully easy. Everything was changed. And, on the evening of his twenty-second birthday, he makes this entry in his journal:

June 12, 1841.—My Birthnight. I have been for the last hour on the sea-shore, not dreaming, but thinking deeply and strongly, and forming determinations which are to affect my life through time and through eternity. Before the sleeping earth and the sleepless sea and stars I have devoted myself to God, a vow never to be recalled.

Of the singular means of his spiritual illumination, Kingsley made no secret. 'He has,' as somebody has said, 'told the lovely story in every book that he wrote; and, to those who knew him well, his every look and every action told it even more emphatically. Some men take pains to conceal their love. It seemed *his* pride to declare it. How often has he said that whatever he has done or achieved was due to the love that came to him in the hour of his deepest crisis, to guide, to strengthen, and to glorify his life.'

V

Love is—God! God is—Love!

Having made this romantic and epoch-making dis-covery on that lovely summer's day, Kingsley found it corroborated everywhere. Turn which way he would, everything seemed to be telling him that *God is love*. He was like a man who, staring with naked eye at the glory of the sun, sees that flaming orb imprinted upon everything on which he afterwards looks. A devoted naturalist, he turned afresh to 'God's great green book,' as he called the open air, and he found the story of the love of God on every page. Nobody in that Hampshire country-side knew better than the rector the fox-earth on the moor, the reedy hover of the pike, the still hole where the chub were to be found. He knew the lore of the beetle, the lizard, and the field-mouse; the shrubs, the wild flowers, and the ferns whispered their secrets to him.

'Everything tells me,' he said, 'that *God is love.*'
And, concerning a young friend in whom he was
particularly interested, he wrote: 'Teach her to love
God; teach her to love Nature. *God is love,* and, the
more we love Him, the more we love everything
about us.' His discovery of the divine love in field
and hedgerow made him natural—a great human—
a man among men. He would discuss the rotation
of crops with the farmers, the hedging and ditching
with the laborers. In preaching his funeral sermon
in Westminster Abbey, Dean Stanley said that 'he
was a layman in the guise of a clergyman—fishing
with the fishermen, hunting with the hunstmen, able
to hold his own in tent and camp, with courtier or
with soldier; an example that a genial companion
may be a Christian gentleman; an evidence that a
clergyman need not be a member of a separate caste
or a stranger to the common interests of his country-
men.' Yet, in all company, Kingsley was true to his
character and to his mission; he made all sorts and
conditions of men admire with him the vastness and
the wonder of the love of God.

He turned to history; became, indeed, Professor
of History at Cambridge University. But one truth
stood out from all others on the horizon of the Past.
'Carlyle's *French Revolution* has,' he writes,
'strengthened my faith in God's righteous government of the world.' 'This,' he declares elsewhere,
'is the real philosophy of history.'

Every path along which his vigorous thought made its way brought him to the same sublime conclusion. He looked back over the providential guidance of his own life. 'It is wonderful,' he murmured; 'surely God is love, *God is love!*' When a young penitent blessed him for his sympathy, he pointed his grateful correspondent in another direction. 'Who am I?' he asked. 'My dear fellow, I went through the same devil's sewer, with a thousand times the teaching and advantages which you have had. Do not thank *me*. If there be pity, affection, patience in men like me, they must have come *from Him.*' Above all, he beheld his text glowing with new grandeur whenever he turned to the Cross. The longer he lived, the more certain he became that the Son of God is the supreme revelation of the love of God. 'No clergyman knows less than I do,' he modestly declared, 'about the working of a parish; but one thing I *do* know—that I have to preach Jesus Christ and Him Crucified; and, in season, out of season, and at all risks, to be instant in *that.*'

Even his wife's love—the choicest treasure that earth held for him—became, more and more distinctly, a sacramental thing to him. Every day he regarded it a little more definitely as an exquisitely beautiful revelation of the higher and holier love from which it sprang.

'*Amavimus: amamus: amabimus,*' he wrote in his death-agony, thinking fondly of the gentle spirit fluttering in the other room. 'We have loved: we love: we shall love.' 'How beautiful *love* is!'

Then, just before the end, he drew his daughter to him and whispered a companion word. 'How beautiful *God* is!' he exclaimed with glowing face.

How beautiful Love is!
How beautiful God is!
Love is—God!
God is—Love!

Yes. '*God is love, and he that dwelleth in love dwelleth in God, and God in him.*'

15

SIM PARIS'S TEXT

Hero of *One Increasing Purpose* by A. S. M. Hutchinson.

Luke 17:21

I

'*Why?*'

That was Sim's problem. It puzzled him; it worried him; it tortured him. He could not sleep at night for thinking about it. And, as the years passed, the question became more insistent and more baffling. Sim—or, to give him his full name, Simon Paris—is the hero of Mr. A. S. M. Hutchinson's *One Increasing Purpose*. Or perhaps he is, in some sense, Mr. Hutchinson himself. Mr. J. C. W. Reith claims to know Mr. Hutchinson as well as it is possible to know him, and he assures us that 'not all the indignant and embarrassed denials of the author would shake my conviction that, in much of the narrative of Simon Paris, he is revealing the deepest and tenderest experiences of his own life and the fullest aspirations of his own heart.' Mr. Hutchinson's Sim has been right through the war from its start with the first expeditionary force to its close with the Armistice; yet he has come through absolutely unscathed! He has never been wounded, never captured, never sick. He has been through desperate fighting; he has been in places where it seemed incredible that he could come out alive; again and again he has been the only survivor. It seemed miraculous. Why was it?

He wished that he could talk it over with his mother. But she is dead. As long as she lived, he always went into her room last thing at night, knelt beside her bed, and had a little talk with her. The kneeling became habitual, almost mechanical. Even after she died he maintained the habit of kneeling down at bedtime for a little talk with mother. During the war the practice had been somewhat interfered with; other men were present; they might think he was praying. But one night he finds himself alone in his dug-out; his two companions have been killed by a shell. The incident intensifies his problem. He throws himself on his knees.

'Why is it, mother?' he cries, in dreadful bitterness of spirit. 'Why, with all these falling around me every day, should *I* be spared?'

He could never explain what happened. He saw nothing, heard nothing. Yet, kneeling in the dug-out, there rushed in upon his mind a conviction that amounted to absolute knowledge. *He had been spared, and would be spared, because he had been selected, reserved, set apart for an especial purpose.* That was it.

II

Yes, that was it. He had been spared for a purpose. But what was that purpose? Here was a new problem, as elusive and baffling as the old one. During the days that followed the war he made this his quest—to discover the purpose for which he had been spared. It imparted a singular gravity to his behavior. He is the same old Sim Paris—gay, light-hearted, generous—and yet there is something different. An odd wistfulness seems to possess him.

'There's *something up* with Simon,' observes his brother Charles; and, at some time or other, almost every character in the book makes a similar remark.

'You've changed a lot somehow, Sim,' says Alice. 'What is it?'

Everybody noticed it. Even those who had not known him before the war remarked that he was not as other men.

'There's *something up* with that chap,' said Lardy Quinnet.

The added seriousness that has come into Sim's character makes him peculiarly attractive to those whose hearts are aching. In the homes of both his brothers there are all the elements of domestic disaster. A time comes when Sim feels that he will discover his purpose more clearly if he leaves London and takes a cottage in the country. The day before he leaves, he runs against Alice—the wife of Charles—in the city. She is laughing; yet there is a look of anguish underneath her gaiety. In reality, she is trembling on the brink of a hideous abyss.

'Oh, Sim,' she says, as she takes his hand in parting, 'I *wish* you were not going. There is a strength about you, Sim, you cannot know; and I——'

Linda, Andrew's wife, comes to see him off at the station. And, oddly enough, she uses the same words. Linda, beautiful and frolicsome, is a born romp. To her, life seems one long jest; laughter lives perpetually upon her lips. But, on the railway platform, Sim sees another Linda. The laughter has vanished from her eyes, the rattle from her tongue. 'Sim,' she exclaims, in a passion of emotion, in the depths of which a great terror seems to lurk, 'Sim, I wish *to God* you were not going!'

In some extraordinary way, Sim's new seriousness makes him the strength of the stumbling and the refuge of the distressed. Yet it is only the seriousness of a quest, a search, a longing. For, although Sim has discovered that he has been spared for a purpose, he is still wondering what that purpose can possibly be.

III

In solving that problem, *three* people help him. Old Yeoman is the *first*. Old Yeoman is the blind carpenter who occupies the cottage that Sim has bought. He is a good old man, who spends his days in carving seats of solid oak and in setting them up on the crests of the steepest hills. And he spends his evenings reading his braille Bible. Sim falls in

love with Old Yeoman. He likes the idea of the
old man spending his last days in fashioning these
oaken resting-places. He likes the inscription that
he carves so cunningly upon the seats. It reads:

REST, PASSER-BY, THEN CHEERILY ON:
PEACE ON THY HABITATION, PASSER-BY!

'Why, Yeoman,' Sim exclaimed one day, 'you
seem to be putting your very soul into those seats.
And why not? Artists express themselves in colors,
sculptors in stone; I don't see why a man shouldn't
express himself in wood!'

'In wood!' replies the old man, 'in wood! It has
been done, sir! Aye, the mightiest expression of a
Man ever the world knew hath been in wood!' And
then he adds reverently, 'The cross of Christ, sir;
the cross of Christ!'

And Sim liked to hear Old Yeoman reading aloud
from his braille Bible. He has read a bit of it every
day for twenty years—ever since his *lightness* came
over him. He always called his blindness his *lightness*. 'My eyes were opened when my eyes were
closed,' he says fondly, as he reaches for the precious
volume. He loves to find *messages* for people by
inserting a paper-knife among the sacred leaves and
reading aloud the words to which it points.

'You had better find me a *message*,' says Sim.

The old man solemnly proceeds to do so.

'One Simon, him they compelled to bear His cross.'

Old Yeoman reads the words in his deep, rich
voice.   Sim is staggered.   His very name!   It is
the first glimmering of his purpose.

IV

Lady England is the *second* person who helps Sim
in his quest.   Sir Henry and Lady England belong
to the old school.   *He* is the typical English country
gentleman; *she* is the typical country lady.   And
they have quaint, old-fashioned notions.   Sunday is
kept strictly but pleasantly.   It is the most restful
and delightful day of the week.   They keep up the
custom of family prayer.   The three maidservants
are called in; they do not sit together, but distribute
themselves among the family; and Sir Henry reads
a passage from the Bible and conducts some prayers.
When it is finished, he crosses to the door, opens it,
and bids each servant good-night as she leaves the
room.

It is a jolly household.   Sim enjoys the society of
the young people immensely.   But the thing that im-
presses him most is their constant references to
K.O.H.   A famous author is one day a guest at the
house.   He tells at table of his recent sojourn in the
French Alps.   His only neighbor was an old woman
who lived in a rude cabin a hundred yards away with
a goat and some chickens.   She smoked a huge
wooden pipe.   'But one particularly vile day,' the

author says, 'knowing that I used to sit, frozen with cold, writing at my table, she came across with a hot brick for me to put my feet on. I thought it the kindest, gentlest action I had come across.'

'Why, that was K.O.H. kindness,' cry the England girls in chorus.

'And,' replies one of the daughters, 'K.O.H. kindnesses are the sort that spring just out of simple goodness of heart—*Kingdom of Heaven* kindness, you know!'

Sim tells them about Old Yeoman. They are delighted.

'You've got the idea exactly,' they said. 'Mother, Major Paris must be given the freedom of the family. He gets our passwords to the T. The idea of seats like that! Yes, that is just what K.O.H. kindness is!'

'The truth is there!' Sim says to himself as he rides home. 'I am positive of it. The inner thing; the thing behind; the positive faith that will satisfy; it is the faith of the K.O.H.; the faith of the spirit of the Kingdom of Heaven! It is there! It is in the K.O.H. spirit that I shall find my purpose!'

V

Elizabeth Glade is the *third* person who helps Sim in his quest. He always felt that she would solve his problem. But where is she? Before he went to the war he had fallen under her spell; but during those confused years he had lost all trace of her. At last he finds her and tells her of his experience.

'Sim,' she says, 'there is a purpose for you. I know it. I am convinced of it.'

He smiles wonderingly.

'Sim,' she continues, 'I believe that it is *of God!*'

This occurs early in the book, before Sim has met Old Yeoman or the Englands. Elizabeth's words startle him.

'I wish,' he writes to her, 'that you had not put that *"of God"* idea into my head. It worries me.' And again: 'I sometimes have a frightened feeling that God is *after me.*'

Poor Elizabeth! She has her own terrible struggle. Her father has betrayed a financial trust; and Elizabeth has vowed that she will never rest, and certainly never marry, until she has restored to Miss Andiron every penny that her dead father has taken. It is a thankless task. One day, with great pride, she takes Miss Andiron a greater sum than usual— sixty-five pounds! Miss Andiron takes the notes, whose number has drawn upon the number of their earner's hours of rest, whose worth has debited the worth of her vitality, whose freshness has paled the freshness of her cheeks. 'I say thank you,' says Miss Andiron, 'because I am polite. Nobody can expect me to be really grateful for the bare return, in small parts, of that of which your father robbed me.' Elizabeth takes grapes and little delicacies to Miss Andiron on occasions; but each time she is told of the abundance of such luxuries that Miss Andiron could have enjoyed if Elizabeth's father had only been honest.

Towards the end of the book, when Sim is thinking over the lesson that he learned in the home of the Englands, a text suddenly flashes into his mind. K.O.H.! K.O.H. kindness! K.O.H. peace! Where is the K.O.H.? And then the words dart in upon his mind: *'The Kingdom of Heaven is within you!'* He tells Elizabeth.

'I have it!' he cries in ecstasy; 'I have it! *"The Kingdom of Heaven is within you!"* In you, Elizabeth; in you; in me; in each of us! Christ within!'

'Oh, Sim,' cries Elizabeth, 'that is your purpose. Make it known! Make it known!'

'I have thought of that,' replies Sim.

VI

Meanwhile, the avalanche of tragedy that has threatened the homes of Sim's brothers has descended. In his wretchedness, Charles commits suicide. The news of his terrible death snatches his wife from the brink of the precipice. Another hour, and she would have whelmed herself in the shame of the adulteress. Her husband knew nothing of that. He died loving and trusting her. It is Sim who breaks to her the tragic news. And, in that bitter hour of self-reproach, it is Sim who comforts her. In the day that is the darkest day of her life, albeit the day of her deliverance from a frightful transgression, Sim is to her a hiding-place from the wind, a covert from the tempest, as rivers of water in a dry place, and as the shadow of a great rock in a weary land.

The crisis swoops down upon Andrew very differently. Andrew loves Linda for her beauty—for *that* and for that alone. And, all at once, poor Linda's loveliness is desolated by small-pox. Not one vestige of her former charm remains; even her silvery voice is thin, dry, metallic. The small-pox is quickly followed by another sickness, almost as serious. Sim is sent for; and, in that cruel crisis, he is everything both to Linda and to Andrew.

'Tell me something good,' pleads Linda.

Sim understands. He talks to her of the Kingdom of Heaven and of the living Christ. He softly recites '*Abide with me.*'

In those days, too, Andrew comes to feel that, in worshipping her beauty alone, he has sinned a great sin against Linda. He pours out his heart to Sim; Sim reciprocates the confidence by telling the story of his purpose and pointing his distressed brother to the Saviour. As a consequence, husband and wife learn to love each other in a new way—in the K.O.H. way.

And Sim? Sim feels that it is his mission in life to make his purpose known. He buys a caravan, and sets out into the world to tell men that the Kingdom of Heaven is neither in the north nor in the south nor in the east nor in the west. *'The Kingdom of Heaven is within you.'* It consists in the enthronement of the Living Saviour in the individual soul. Wherever Sim goes, the crowds flock to welcome his vital message. They call him 'The Man with the Lamp'; and the rays of that Lamp shine with gladdening radiance across the entire country.

16

St. Patrick's Text

A.D. c. 389–c. 461
Celtic missionary to Ireland.

Philippians 1:21

I

I ALWAYS feel tempted to wear a little sprig of green in my buttonhole on St. Patrick's Day. And if I could satisfy myself that my behavior, in doing so, would be construed as a personal tribute to St. Patrick—only that and nothing more—I should certainly yield to that annual impulse.

For St. Patrick has always been one of my heroes. As a child I gloried in the story of his romantic boyhood in my own land; I loved the thrilling tale of his capture by the pirates and of his being sold into slavery in Ireland; and I revelled in the particulars of his adventurous escape.

It stirs one's blood to think of the age in which he lived. It was the age of the Goth and the Vandal and the Hun. Indeed, it was because these mighty iconoclasts were thundering at the gates of Rome that the forces of the Empire had to be withdrawn from Britain. And, in their absence, the freebooters swept down upon the unprotected coasts and carried poor Patrick and his playmates away into captivity.

It was a great age, too, in the Church—the age of

Jerome and Chrysostom and Ambrose and Augustine. And Patrick was destined to impart to that golden age an additional lustre. For he harnessed all the scholarship of the Church and all the devotion of the Church and all the wealth of the Church to a sublime purpose. He made the Church a Missionary Church—a Church that sent its flaming heralds into every land.

From the days of the apostles to the days of the Reformation, the Church produced no preacher or teacher who, for fervor, passion, and intensity, can compare with St. Patrick. His love for Christ was a fire that burned in his bones day and night. He is one of the most ardent, one of the most vehement, one of the most fervid spirits of all time.

II

I am writing on March 17. With unbounded satisfaction and delight I have been celebrating St. Patrick's Day. I do not mean that I participated in the procession in the morning or that I competed in the sports in the afternoon. Truth to tell, I am tortured by a doubt as to whether processions and sports would have been much to the taste of St. Patrick himself. In my own quiet way, however, I entered heart and soul into the commemoration, and, in the years to come, shall never fail to keep the feast.

Here in Australia, St. Patrick's Day comes to us amidst a rustle of autumn leaves. This year it was one of those rich and cloudless days that sometimes visit us just as summer is mellowing to its close. A deck-chair stood upon the lawn, coaxing me into the clear sunshine and bracing autumn air. I took with me all the biographies I could collect—both Catholic and Protestant—and all the books that were likely to contain references to St. Patrick. During the next hour or two my felicity was complete. For the first time in my life I felt that I really knew St. Patrick. I looked with reverent admiration upon his spare form and slightly stooping figure; I gazed long and intently into those flashing eyes in which the fires of a quenchless enthusiasm seemed to be always burning. After reading for awhile, it seemed to me that St. Patrick had drawn up his chair and was seated at my side. The words that met my eyes upon the printed page seemed to be falling from his very lips, and were uttered in a voice that quivered with subdued intensity and quiet passion. He told me of his wayward boyhood and of the dramatic crisis which led to his conversion.

III

'There were three of us—boys of about sixteen,' he said. 'It was a hot summer's evening. Having bathed in the breakers as they rushed up the long sweep of crescent beach, we had amused ourselves by chasing each other over the huge piles of massive rock that mark Bannaventa's wild, romantic shore. And then, the twilight falling, we sprawled in the mouth of a large cave and completed our arrangements for an escapade that we were planning for the following day. Suddenly a party of fierce-looking men rushed out from behind the headland. We sprang to our feet and attempted to fly, but found our retreat cut off by others of the same party, into whose arms we incontinently rushed. These Irish freebooters soon bound us, hand and foot, and carried us to their ship. Within the next few hours hundreds of others—the young men and maidens of Bannaventa and its neighboring villages—were brought on board. Most of us were in tears. And thus, in my seventeenth year, I was carried away captive into Ireland. When, after a miserable voyage, the ship reached her destination, we were marched across the country in chains. And there, in Connaught—famished, exhausted, homesick, and utterly wretched—we were sold into bondage; and for six years I endured the unspeakable horrors of slavery.'

St. Patrick hung his fine head for a moment as these agonizing memories took possession of his mind. After a period of silence, however, he continued his entrancing story.

'Yet,' he went on, 'it was whilst I ate the bitter

bread of that hateful servitude in a foreign land that the light divine broke upon my benighted soul. I called to remembrance the holy things that I had been taught in my dear old home at Bannaventa—things that had there seemed of no account to me. And, by means of those tender memories, the Lord opened my hard and unbelieving heart to a tardy remembrance of my transgressions and led me to turn with my whole soul to my Redeemer.'

St. Patrick went on to tell me of his sensational escape from slavery, of his travels on the Continent, and of the dedication of his life to the work of the ministry. For more than twenty years he persistently contemplated a noble revenge. Although he could not think of Ireland without a shudder, he bravely resolved to return as a missionary to the people who had enslaved him.

'I seemed,' he exclaimed, with evident feeling, 'I seemed to hear the voices of those who dwelt near the forest of Focluth, and they cried out in unison, begging me to return to them. And my heaart was melted within me, and I prayed that I might even yet be permitted to carry the gospel to those among whom I had toiled in captivity.'

The years came and went; the opportunity never occurred; yet St. Patrick never relinquished his dream. 'His eyes,' says Father Morris, 'ever followed the sun as it set over the western sea, and he thought of those forests of Ireland from whence came the cry of the little ones who asked for the bread of life and there was none to break it to them. Youth passed away, and maturity, and the silver had begun to creep into his hair before the day broke for which he had yearned so long.' At length, however, he was made a bishop, with Ireland as his see. His joy knew no bounds. 'In his humility,' Father Morris says again, 'he called himself an ignorant sinner, a fool, and the rudest and least among the faithful; but, when he spoke in the name of his Lord, his faith gave him majesty and authority, and he became in very truth that which he announced himself to be—the Ambassador of Jesus Christ.'

But I did not mean to quote from books, however excellent. Let me return to St. Patrick as I saw him —or seemed to see him—on the lawn. It was, he said, very wonderful to him that one who had stained his soul with so many iniquities should have been called to evangelize a great people across the seas.

'I am greatly a debtor to God,' he exclaimed with deep emotion. 'What have I done to deserve the grace that has been so bountifully bestowed upon me? When I think of the multitudes who have been born again through my instrumentality, and when I think of the vast numbers of these converts whom the Lord has called to be missionaries and evangelists, I am bowed down with penitence and adoring gratitude. His grace has been wonderful, most wonderful!'

IV

'And now,' he added, rising and pacing the green grass at my feet, 'and now, for me, *life is Christ: life is Christ!'*

The words appeared to spring so naturally and spontaneously from his hot heart and fervent lips that I did not recognize till afterwards that he had but quoted a text. The words have been upon my mind ever since, however, and I shall never hear or quote that text again without thinking of St. Patrick.

'For me to live is Christ'—so runs the passage in our Authorized Version.

'Life means Christ to me'—So Dr. Moffatt renders it.

'For, to me, life is Christ'—it is thus that Dean Alford translates the phrase, using the very words of St. Patrick. 'It means,' adds the Dean, 'that all my life, all my energy, all my time, is His—I live Christ!'

Christ is Life—in those three words the whole of the evangelical message is comprehended.

Life is Christ—in those same words the entire imperative of Christian experience and service is summed up.

In pursuing these researches I lost the vivid sense of St. Patrick's personality and presence; but he had conveyed a message to my mind that will linger there as long as life endures.

V

As we sat together on the lawn, St. Patrick fastened upon my mind one indelible impression. He shamed by easy-going torpor by his consuming earnestness. His presence seemed to scorch me. I can understand now the extraordinary contagion of his faith. It spread like wildfire. 'It was,' says one historian, 'an age of wonders, when grace was given without measure; it was a time of intellectual and spiritual development so rapid and so universal that the record reads like an invention of the imagination rather than a sober statement of facts.' Ireland was transformed. Jocelyn declares that there was no desert, no solitude, no hiding-place in the island, however remote, that did not feel the vital breath of that beneficent revival; 'and so,' he adds, 'Ireland came to be distinguished throughout the whole world by the extraordinary title of the Island of Saints!'

Every great movement takes to itself something of the personality of the man who leads it. It was inevitable that the Church that sprang up under the hand of St. Patrick should be a Church marked by the most intense missionary fervor.

'For me, life is Christ!' cried St. Patrick.

'For me, life is Christ!' cried each of his converts.

The world has never known a Church more charged with evangelistic passion than the Irish Church of those days. In his *Short History of the*

English People, J. R. Green speaks of the phenomenal success of St. Patrick. His message was received, he says, with a great burst of popular
enthusiasm. And then the historian adds a striking
sentence. 'The new Christian life,' he says, 'beat
too strongly to brook confinement within the bounds
of Ireland itself. Irish missionaries swarmed across
the seas. Irish Christianity flung itself with a fiery
zeal into battle with that mass of heathenism that
was rolling in upon the world.' In those days—the
days of Alaric and Attila and Genseric—Goths and
Huns and Vandals were threatening the very
foundations of civilization; and the Irish Church—
the Church of St. Patrick—was one of the most
potent forces in preserving the sanctity and integrity
of the social fabric.

Preaching from the pulpit of Westminster Abbey
some time ago, Dr. J. B. Crozier, Archbishop of
Armagh, declared that St. Patrick was one of the
master-missionaries of all time. If justice were done,
he said, St. Patrick would be recognized, not only as
the Apostle of Ireland, but as the Apostle of England and of Scotland too.

'Walk through Britain,' exclaimed the archbishop,
'from the Thames to the Tweed, from Lindisfarne
to Iona, and ask from whom did it receive the gospel.
And you hear that it was from Irish missionaries—
St. Patrick, St. Columba, and their successors.
Cross over to France and extend your journey to

Cologne, and ask the people to tell you who first
evangelized their forefathers. They will tell you it
was St. Kilian, an Irish missionary. Pass on to
Wurtzburgh, and you will get the same reply. In
Salzburgh the citizens will tell you that their fathers
first learned of Christ from Virgil, the Irish bishop.
Pass on to Batavia, Friesland, and Westphalia,
mount the Alps and climb into the heart of Switzer-
land, and ten thousand voices will echo from the hills
and valleys the name of St. Gall, a missionary from
Ireland. And when you come home again, St.
Aidan in the north, and St. Germoc in the south,
with the many saints to whom the stalls in Truro
Cathedral are dedicated, will remind you of what
England owes to St. Patrick and his followers.'

The dinner-bell rang, summoning me to leave the
lawn. But I had learned my lesson. My apathy had
been rebuked by the consuming zeal of a great soul
in deadly earnest. Moreover, I had discovered that
the ardor of my exalted guest was the ardor, not
of partisanship, nor of fanaticism, but of profound
personal affection. His fervor was the fervor of the
lover; for St. Patrick was passionately in love with
the Saviour by whom he had been so wonderfully
redeemed.

VI

Before he left me, he recited to me some stanzas
of his immortal *Breastplate*—the poem by means of

which, to most of us, he is best known.   And, after
all, it is merely his text set to music.

> I bind to myself this day
> The Power of His Incarnation,
> The Power of His Crucifixion,
> The Power of His Resurrection,
> With His Ascension.
>
> Christ be with me, Christ within me,
>   Christ behind me, Christ before me,
> Christ beside me, Christ to win me,
>   Christ to comfort and restore me;
> Christ beneath me, Christ above me,
>   Christ in quiet, Christ in danger,
> Christ in hearts of all that love me,
>   Christ in mouth of friend and stranger.

Christ is—Life!—that was the startling discovery
of St. Patrick's youth.

Life is—Christ!—that was the growing experience of his later, richer, and most fruitful years.

Life is Christ!   To love Christ!   To preach
Christ!   To live Christ!

It is thus that I have kept St. Patrick's Day: and
the felicitous and fragrant memory of the celebra-
tion will not readily fade from my mind.

17

JOSEPH ADDISON'S TEXT
1672–1719
English essayist, hymn writer, and statesman.

Psalm 23

I

THE merry month of May had broken upon England
with blue skies and sparkling sunshine. In the tiny
hamlet of Milston the May Day revels were at their
height when it was whispered among the happy
villagers that a baby had just been born in the
thatched old parsonage near by. The young men
and maidens who danced around the maypole on
that Wiltshire green little dreamed that the child
who had just made his advent in the dreamy old
house among the elms was destined to effect one of
the most notable transformations in his country's
history: to wield an authority so absolute that it
would be said of him that he could have had the
crown for the asking; and to be remembered with
honor and gratitude by generations yet unborn.

Yet, less than fifty years later, the baby who was
born amidst the sunshine and the laughter of those
May Day frolics is buried at dead of night amidst
a nation's lamentations. By the ghostly light of
torches and tapers he is borne to his resting-place in
the stately Abbey.

How silent do his old companions tread
  By midnight lamps the mansions of the dead,
Thro' breathing statues, then unheeded things,
  Thro' rows of warriors and thro' walks of kings!

A century later still a fine statue is erected to his memory in Poets' Corner. The monument is inscribed *to the noblest purifier of our literature.* 'Such a mark of national respect was due to this unsullied statesman, to this accomplished scholar, to this master of pure English eloquence, to this consummate painter of life and manners,' says Lord Macaulay. The essay, in which Macaulay admits that his admiration for Addison verges dangerously on idolatry, was written in 1843; and when, sixteen years later, Macaulay himself was borne to the Abbey for burial, he was interred at the foot of the Addison statue. He himself would have coveted no resting-place more honorable.

II

A quiet, thoughtful, white-haired boy—as reflective as Milton and as timid as Cowper—Addison had the genius to perceive that there was a great work waiting to be done in the world; and he had the practical sagacity and intellectual energy to brace himself for the enterprise. At the dawn of the eighteenth century English standards and English manners were at their lowest ebb. Politics had de-

generated into an undignified squabble; society was
as corrupt as it could very well be; music, art, and
literature were all degraded; the sports and pastimes
of life were universally squalid and usually obscene;
religion itself had become formal, sanctimonious,
and largely hypocritical. 'Even the saint,' says
Addison, 'was of a sorrowful countenance, and
generally eaten up with spleen and melancholy.' The
number of people who saw anything to be deplored
in all this was extremely small; but, of that select
company, Joseph Addison was a distinguished member.

He saw clearly that things were capable of im-
provement; and, like the architect of a new era, he
carefully drafted his plans. He aspired to be the
apostle of Christian cheerfulness and clean mirth.
In one of the earliest numbers of the *Spectator* he
says that he intends to enliven morality with wit and
to temper wit with morality. Since our little race
began, many men have embarked upon an attempt
to straighten a perverse and crooked world; but very
few of them have had the satisfaction of reviewing
their enterprise with any marked degree of exulta-
tion. Addison's ideal was, however, realized in its
entirety. He lived a life of stainless integrity; he
endeared himself by his courtesy, chivalry, and
modesty to the greatest men of his time; he held,
through thick and thin, to his early resolves and
aspirations; and he won for himself a name which

men of all ranks and of all parties unfeignedly delighted to honor.

III

And he achieved all this in defiance of the heaviest
possible handicap.   He was afflicted by the most excruciating bashfulness.   Like Shelley, he could never
enter a drawing-room without falling over a chair
nor cross a lawn in company without tripping over
his own feet.   His agonizing timidity was the bane
of his life.   He loved good company and lively dis-
cussion; nothing pleased him better than to stretch
out his legs and talk; he was a very prince among
coffee-house men.   In his day the coffee-houses
were in the hey-day of their illustrious career.   A
galaxy of the most eminent statesmen and scholars
of his time would sit with him until the dawn came
stealing through the windows; he would hold them
entranced hour after hour; and when at last the company broke up, it broke up with a sigh.   Yet if, at
any moment, the door opened and a strange face
appeared, the sparkling conversationalist shrank into
instant silence; shyness paralyzed the tongue; and
his obvious discomfort threw a pitiable awkwardness
over his entire behavior.

He became a Member of Parliament, and even a
Cabinet Minister; yet he was too nervous to address
the House.   If he could have talked at Westminster

as he talked at Button's Coffee-house, he would have bequeathed to posterity a reputation that would have eclipsed the shining records of Pitt, Fox, Sheridan, and Burke. But it was impossible. Just once he rose in his place; stammered out one or two broken and incoherent sentences; blushed, coughed, apologized, sat down; and never ventured on a second attempt. Yet he held several important portfolios. In that respect his case is quite unique. Macaulay attributes his political ascendancy to two causes. In days in which parliamentary speeches were not reported, and in which the orator could hope to influence none but those who actually heard his voice, a Prime Minister was glad to have in his Cabinet a man who, by the skilful use of his pen, could lay the case for the Government before the country in pamphlets as cogent and convincing as those written by Addison. And any Prime Minister in any age would be glad to have in his Cabinet a man in whose unimpeachable integrity and untarnished honor the English people had such implicit confidence as they had in Addison. For, in spite of his defects as a speaker, Addison was the most trusted statesman of his time.

IV

Addison was the natural successor of the Puritans. He was a Puritan in an age that had repudiated Puritanism. Milton and Bunyan were the last of the

Puritans. Addison was a child of two when Milton died: he was sixteen when Bunyan passed away. Twelve years before his birth, the Restoration had swept Puritanism into oblivion. Paradise was lost. Addison determined to recapture some of the treasure that had been abandoned in the general overthrow; he resolved to re-establish something of the golden tradition that had been blurred by the great reaction.

'I will *purify* English life and English letters!' exclaims this young Puritan, as, a boy in a rural hamlet, he looks out of his lattice window upon a crooked world.

'The noblest *purifier* of our literature!' says the inscription at the Abbey.

The word occurs repeatedly in every estimate of his life and influence. Addison's career is an epic of purity. We are told again and again of the purity of his life, of the purity of his motives, of the purity of his conceptions, of the purity of his wit, and of the purity of his style.

Now, the question arises: Whence came this passion for purity? The influence of Addison is like a clear and silvery stream pouring itself into the life of the nation, cleansing and sweetening everything that it touches. In what mountain tarn or wooded dell did this translucent stream have its source, its origin, its fountain-head?

And, to answer that question, we must return to

Milston. And here, in the old parsonage among the elms, I see the boy sitting at his mother's knee, learning his evening lesson.

'I'm so tired, mother,' he pleads, 'so tired and sleepy! Let me say my favorite lesson to-night; don't make me learn anything new!'

She yields to his persuasion and he repeats the words that possess a singular fascination for him. He is never too tired for *their* recital.

'*The Lord is my shepherd; I shall not want,*' he begins; and, without a single slip, makes his way through the Psalm till, looking into his mother's face with a sleepy smile, he concludes: '*And I will dwell in the house of the Lord for ever.*'

He learned the words, innocently and thoughtlessly, at his mother's knee; but they became the song, the strength, and the solace of his later life; and he was still crooning them to himself when he turned his back to the world and his face to the wall.

V

There were two things of which Joseph Addison was passionately fond. He never tired of the woods and the fields and the streams of Wiltshire, and he never tired of the twenty-third Psalm. The two things blended into one, for, little by little, he came to associate the imagery of his Psalm with the landscapes that he loved so well. To him the *green pas-*

tures were the Wiltshire fields, the *still waters* were the Wiltshire streams, and the *sheep* of the Psalm were the flocks that grazed on the graceful slopes around him. In the course of a recent visit to the Homeland, I found myself, one lovely afternoon, exploring the villages among which Joseph Addison spent his boyhood. Out on the Salisbury Plains we gathered scabious, harebells, antirrhinums, and scarlet poppies; and, as we did so, a pair of owls, that had been sitting beside the road, fluttered past almost within reach of our hands. Then, resuming our journey, we passed through Amesbury, where Addison went to school, and proceeded to the Druid ruins at Stonehenge. 'No one,' says Mr. W. J. Courthope, in his *Life of Addison*, 'no one who has travelled on a summer's day across Salisbury Plain, with its vast canopy of sky, and its open tracts of undulating downland, relieved by no shadows, except such as are thrown by the passing clouds, the grazing sheep, and the great circle of Stonehenge, will forget the delightful sense of refreshment and repose produced by the descent into the valley of the Avon. The sounds of human life rising from the villages after the long solitude of the plain, the shade of the deep woods, and the coolness of the clear and tranquil river, are equally delicious to the sense and the imagination.' And Mr. Courthope closes the paragraph by expressing his conviction that these lovely scenes rushed back upon the mind of Addison when

he composed his paraphrase of the Psalm of which
he was so fond.

> The Lord my pasture shall prepare,
> And feed me with a shepherd's care;
> His presence shall my wants supply,
> And guard me with a watchful eye;
> My noonday walks He shall attend,
> And all my midnight hours defend.
>
> When in the sultry glebe I faint,
> Or on the thirsty mountain pant,
> To fertile vales and dewy meads
> My weary, wandering steps He leads,
> Where peaceful rivers, soft and slow,
> Amid the verdant landscape flow.

And just as the Wiltshire scenery lent a beauty to
the Psalm, so the Psalm, in its turn, imparted an
added charm to the scenery. In one of his three
essays on *Cheerfulness* he tells us that the joyousness
of his faith made every prospect more pleasing. 'It
consecrates every field and wood,' he says; 'it turns
an ordinary walk into a morning or evening sacrifice; it improves every transient gleam of joy into
an inviolable and perpetual state of happiness and
bliss.'

As a boy, Addison had been horrified by the
gloomy aspect which religion usually assumed. The
saint was the victim of an abiding melancholy.
Addison found a sunnier faith—a faith that matched
the rich verdure of his Wiltshire fields and the bright
sparkle of his Wiltshire streams—and he found it

in the twenty-third Psalm. 'The piety of Addison,
says Macaulay, 'was of a singularly cheerful character. He loved the Psalm which represents the
Ruler of all things under the endearing image of a
shepherd, whose crook guides the flock through
gloomy and desolate glens to meadows well watered
and rich in herbage. God was to him the all-wise
and all-powerful Friend who had watched over his
cradle with more than maternal tenderness; who had
listened to his cries before they could form themselves in prayer; who had preserved his youth from
the snares of vice; who had made his cup run over
with worldly blessings; and who had doubled the
value of those blessings by bestowing a thankful
heart to enjoy them. To that goodness he ascribed
all the happiness of his life, and on that goodness he
relied in the hour of death with the love that casteth
out fear.'

As he lay dying, his generous heart and sensitive
conscience led him to crave the forgiveness of his
friends for wrongs which they had never noticed
or had long since forgotten. And then, at peace with
all the world, he abandoned himself to the enjoyment
of that special realization of the divine presence
which his Psalm assured to him. *'Ye, though I
walk through the valley of the shadow of death, I
will fear no evil, for Thou art with me.'* Nor did
the promise fail. Near the end, his son-in-law, the
Earl of Warwick, stood beside his bed. 'See,' ex-

claimed the patient, 'in what perfect peace a Christian can die!' 'He taught us,' says Tickell in his elegy,

> He taught us how to live and (oh! too high
> The price of knowledge) taught us how to die!

His pilgrimage was over. Goodness and mercy had followed him all the days of his life. As he passed through the Valley of the Shadow of Death, the rod and the staff comforted him. And he had gone to dwell in the House of the Lord for ever.

VI

And Joseph Addison is only one of thousands who, in life and in death, have leaned hard upon the twenty-third Psalm and found its support all-sufficient. 'This Psalm of serene faith and lofty hope has,' says Mr. Moffat Scott, 'wrought moral miracles, making weak men strong and strong men brave and triumphant. George Herbert, Joseph Addison, Sir Henry Baker, and Heinrich Heine have, in their admiration for it, translated it into immortal verse; it was the first Psalm that John Ruskin learned at his pious mother's knee; St. Francis of Assisi, bareheaded and barefooted, marching forth to convert the Sultan and the Saracens, chanted it in his lonely pilgrimage of love; Nash, the son-in-law of Knox, and the first graduate of the University of Edinburgh, sang it when he left his native shore for exile in France; Marion Harvie, a servant-girl of twenty, sang it on her way to the scaffold at Edinburgh in 1681; and, with the words of this Psalm upon their lips, Edward Irving, the famous London preacher, and Alexander Duff, the great Indian missionary, gave up their souls to God.'

Nor need Mr. Moffat Scott have paused here. For the time would fail to tell of John Wesley, who, on February 10, 1751, finding himself in too great pain to preach on any other theme, found it easy to kneel in his pulpit and expound the beauties of the twenty-third Psalm; or of Bishop Hooper, who, in his 'vile and stinking chamber' in the Fleet prison, resting on his 'little pad of rotten straw,' spends his ebbing strength in writing an exposition of the Shepherd Psalm; or of the Empress Eugénie, who, on receiving the tragic news of the disaster at Sedan, takes shelter in a hotel at Ryde and is comforted by reading in the Bible that she finds there, *'The Lord is my shepherd';* or of Daniel Webster, who, when he closes his eyes for the last time, asks that the Psalm about *the rod and the staff* may be read to him. Or of Augustine and Luther and Lowell, and a great host of others, who, in the hour of need, have shared with Joseph Addison the raptures and consolations of his Psalm.

VII

I know a young mother. She was teaching a tiny toddler the twenty-third Psalm.

'Now say *this* after me,' she said: ' "*The Lord is my shepherd."* '

'*The Lord is your shepherd,*' the baby lips replied.

'No; no! Not *your* shepherd, but *my* shepherd,' exclaimed the mother.

'That's what I said, mum; *the Lord is your shepherd,*' repeated the little one.

And the poor young mother had to give it up for that night, feeling crestfallen and disappointed.

I know a padre—the Rev. J. A. Gault, O.B.E.—who did wonderful work in France. It was his custom, when men were going into the firing-line, to get them to repeat with him the opening clause of the Shepherd Psalm, ticking it off on the fingers of their left hands. The little finger represented the word *The;* the next finger, *Lord;* the middle finger, *is;* the index finger, *my;* and the thumb, *shepherd.* Every man was asked to mark the palm of his hand with indelible pencil to remind him of the text, and special stress was laid on the index finger—*my* shepherd—the finger that spoke of the personal appropriation of the shepherdly care. After the battle of Bullecourt, one of Mr. Gault's young fellows was found, quite dead, grasping firmly with his right hand the *index finger* of his left.

'Don't say *your:* say *my!*' pleaded the puzzled mother. But the tiny tot did not understand.

But Mr. Gault's young soldier understood. And, with Joseph Addison and a host of saints and heroes and martyrs, he rejoiced that he had a place peculiarly his own in the heart of the Good Shepherd, and he clung to that sweet faith in perfect serenity to the last.

18

ELIZABETH FRY'S TEXT
1780–1845
English Quaker philanthropist and prison reformer.

Luke 7:36–50

I

A VERY queenly Quaker was Elizabeth Fry. 'She was,' the Duke of Argyll assures us, 'a most majestic woman—the only human being I have ever met whom I felt to be really very great. You realized instinctively that she would never disappoint you.' Tall, and well formed, and extremely handsome, with a face of singular sweetness and delicacy, she always bore herself with superb dignity and subtle charm. 'To see her was to love her,' as a bluff old sailor expressively put it. He expected to find her sanctimonious and unco guid. But, on meeting her, he capitulated unconditionally. 'Who,' he asks, 'can resist this beautiful, persuasive, and heavenly-minded woman? To see her is to love her, and to hear her is like listening to the voice of an angel.' There were thousands in England—the highest of the high and the lowest of low low—who would have been glad to accept the old sailor as their spokesman. He expressed their sentiments most perfectly.

Sydney Smith declared that the most sublime

spectacle in modern history was the spectacle of this
fascinating and cultured woman reading the story of
redeeming love to the prisoners of Newgate.   And
Thomas Carlyle entirely agreed with him.   'To see,'
says Sydney Smith, 'to see this noble woman, in the
midst of those wretched and repulsive prisoners; to
see them soothed by the softness of her voice, animated by the fondness of her look, and clinging wor-
shipfully to her as the only being who ever loved
them, this is a sight which breaks down the pageant
of the world; it is the most affecting spectacle which
any human being ever witnessed.'   'She looked,'
says Carlyle, 'like a little spot of purity in a great
swelling mass of corruption.   It was a most moving
thing.   Every word that she uttered in those sweet,
silvery tones of hers went from her heart to the
inmost hearts of her hearers.'   Elizabeth Fry found
a way of her own of making history, and the world
has become a kindlier place in consequence.

II

And yet there was a time when the strait and
sombre Quakers of the eighteenth century looked
with the gravest suspicion on poor Betsy Gurney,
the sprightly and vivacious girl who was destined to
be known to fame as Elizabeth Fry.   For Betsy was
the soul of gaiety.   A born romp, she was the ring-
leader in every frolic.   In *Felix Holt* George Eliot
couples the names of Elizabeth Fry and Santa

Teresa. The two *women*—the English Quakeress
and the Spanish nun—would have been like David
and Jonathan; but the two *girls* would have been
a pretty pair of madcaps. On one occasion, Betsy
organized her sisters into a band of highwaymen,
and they 'held up' the Norwich coach! Her merry
and infectious laughter pealed through the house.
'You can always find Betsy,' somebody said, 'for, if
she isn't laughing, she's humming or whistling or
singing.' She was fond of music, fond of dancing,
fond of gay company, fond of fine horses, and—as
she herself confesses—just a little fond of flirting!
Worst of all in that drab and demure Quaker atmosphere, she was particularly fond of pretty dresses.
Bright colors possessed a rare fascination for her.
A servant who saw Betsy's dashing figure approaching the gate hurried to her mistress and announced
'a beautiful young lady on horseback in a scarlet
riding-habit.' A scarlet riding-habit. Poor Betsy!

Yes, those eighteenth-century Quakers felt very
uncertain about Betsy. And, little as they suspected
it, Betsy felt very uncertain about herself! It did
not occur to those who thought her frivolous that a
serious mind may lurk behind a laughing face, or
that a wonderfully hungry heart may flutter beneath
the bright folds of a scarlet riding-habit. If only
they could have peeped into Betsy's private journal!
They would have found this entry, written at the
age of sixteen:

January, 1797.— My mind is in so dark a state that I see everything through a black medium.

And this, six months later :

July 18, 1797.—I am a bubble, a fool—idle, dissipated, stupid—all outside and no inside—merely a contemptible fine lady, I feel like a ship out at sea without a pilot. I am now seventeen; and if some great and kind circumstance does not happen to me, I shall have my talents devoured by moth and rust, and they will prove a curse instead of a blessing. Dreaded day!

In those days Betsy dreamed, night after night, that she was among the rocks on a lonely shore, hemmed in by the tide. The waters rose to her knees, to her waist, to her shoulders; and then, just as she was actually drowning, she awoke!

But the onlookers who thought our pretty Betsy vain and giddy, never saw that secret diary, and knew nothing of those dreadful dreams. They little suspected the storm that was raging beneath that smiling exterior! And even Betsy herself, longing for *'some great and kind circumstance'* that shall transform her life, never imagines that this sublime circumstance is so near!

III

The *'great and kind circumstance'* took a human form. William Savery, an American Quaker, came to preach at Norwich, and Betsy, with her sisters, went to hear him. As a rule, Betsy found the Quaker meetings unconscionably tedious, and was extremely restless. And on this occasion there would have been some excuse for weariness, for William Savery thought nothing of speaking for two hours and a half. But, to the astonishment of her sisters, she sits spellbound. She had amused the others by going to the meeting in purple shoes, laced with scarlet! Yet, whilst Mr. Savery is preaching, tears course down her cheeks, and she cries most of the way home!

Betsy's diary is, of course, full of it; and, thirty years afterwards, she reverts to the memorable theme. 'That was the casting die in my life,' she says; 'my understanding was opened to receive the truth. At this most critical period, the tender mercy of my God was marvellously displayed towards me. Can any one doubt that it was His Spirit which manifested to me the evil in my own heart; as well as that which I perceived around me, leading me to abhor it and to hunger and thirst after Himself and His righteousness, and after that salvation which cometh by Christ?'

It was then, her sister says, that Betsy awoke to a new life in Christ Jesus. After that eventful day she never again dreamed that she was drowning among the rocks. She had reached a foothold beyond the reach of the devouring tide.

Nor, after that, do we read any more of scarlet

riding-habits or of purple shoes with scarlet laces!
Slowly and very reluctantly, Betsy gave up her
pretty frocks. Little by little the gay tints vanish
from her garments as the vivid hues die out of the
clouds after sunset. I catch a glimpse of her soon
after her conversion, in 'a dainty white gown that
perfectly fits her beautifully proportioned figure.
Her fine flaxen hair is simply combed and parted in
front. She looks peculiarly lovely.' A few months
later I see her, at the age of nineteen, in a plain slate-
colored silk dress; but, as a concession to her girlish
love of stylish things, a black lace veil is twisted into
her long blonde hair in the turban fashion then prev-
alent, the ends hanging on one side. At twenty she
marries Joseph Fry; and, from that time forward,
she is every inch a Quaker.

IV

Elizabeth Fry was thirty-three years of age, and
the mother of eight children (with three more to
come), when she suddenly confronted her destiny.
By this time she had developed an extraordinary gift
for reading the Scriptures. Her elocution was
natural and unstudied; but it was absolutely faultless. Ministers of all denominations came to hear
her, in the hope of discovering her secret. 'Never,'
says the Rev. C. Taylor, 'never have I heard any one
read as Elizabeth Fry read. The solemn reverence

of her manner; the articulation, so exquisitely modu-
lated, so distinct, that not a word of that sweet and
touching voice could fail to be heard. While she
read, her mind appeared to be intensely absorbed in
the passage of Scripture and in nothing else. She
seemed to take in to her own spirit the words which
she read, and to apply them to herself.' Every word
has all the wealth of her own great soul behind it.

Conscious of the value of this rare gift, she wisely
resolves to make the most of it. She reads to her
children and their friends gathered in her drawing-
room; she reads to select parties assembled on her
lawn; she reads to the sick—rich and poor—in
homes and hospitals; she reads to her Quaker companions, who elect her a 'minister.' She reads to the
motley company assembled in the spacious sitting-
room of a wayside inn. From the most unlikely
sources she receives pressing invitations to exercise
her gift. She visits the gipsy encampments in the
lane and holds the wanderers captive as she reads
and talks with them. And then she hears the news
that straightway lures her forth on her life's supreme
adventure.

A Quaker who has visited Newgate horrifies her
by describing the loathsome conditions under which
the prisoners live. Felons, and even untried sus-
pects, are treated like wild beasts. Are they not the
enemies of society? Who cares what tortures they
endure? No degradation is too vile to be imposed

upon them. Mrs. Fry sickens as she listens to the
appalling story, and resolves to do something towards mitigating the horror of the prisoner's lot.
She goes to Newgate. The governor warns her of
the peril of entering the apartment in which the
prisoners are herded together. Nothing daunted,
she persists in her request, and, entering the horrid
dungeon, she beholds a sight that haunts her fancy
like a nightmare to her dying day.

Thus began a work that constituted itself one of
the wonders of the nineteenth century. Crabbe, the
poet, expresses the feeling that most people
cherished:

> One I beheld, a wife, a mother, go
> To gloomy scenes of wickedness and woe!
> She sought her way through all things vile and base,
> And made a prison a religious place:
> Fighting her way—the way angels fight
> With powers of darkness—to let in the light.
> Yet she is tender, delicate, and nice,
> And shrinks from all depravity and vice;
> Shrinks from the ruffian gaze, the savage gloom,
> That reign where guilt and misery find a home;
> Yet all she braved; she kept her steadfast eye
> On the dear cause, and brushed the baseness by.

'On her second visit'—so runs the record—'she
was left alone among the prisoners for some hours.
She read to them several passages of Scripture, and
made a few observations on Christ having come to
save sinners, even those who might be said to have

wasted the greater part of their lives estranged from Him. Some asked who Christ was; others feared that their day of salvation was past.'

Her work took her from prison to prison; from town to town; and even from country to country. 'Wherever she went, she was sure to be found in the sad abodes of the criminal and the suffering, speaking, in her own tones of incomparable pathos and beauty, of that Redeemer who had come to seek and to save the lost.' She was often invited to confer with the authorities concerning suggested improvements; and she everywhere assembled the ladies to point out to them the valuable help that it was in their power to render.

V

During the next few years we catch glimpses of her in all sorts of places and among all sorts of people. She is often at Newgate. Thanks to many eminent artists and authors, we all seem to have seen her there. We have looked into that calm Madonna face, surmounted by its plain, borderless Quaker cap; we have admired that stately, regal figure, garbed in its drab-colored silk cloak; and we have listened to that silvery but solemn voice, which seems to emphasize the wonderful winsomeness of its sublime message.

'By this time,' says her daughter, 'Newgate has

become almost a show. The statesman and the peer, the city functionary and the foreign traveller, the high-bred squire and the country clergyman, flocked to witness the astounding transformation that had passed over the scene.' 'I dined on Saturday,' says Sir James Mackintosh, 'at Devonshire House. The company included the Duke of Norfolk, Lords Lansdowne, Lauderdale, Albemarle, Cowper, Hardwicks, Carnarvon, Sefton, Ossulston, Milton, Duncannon, and others. We discussed Mrs. Fry's exhortation to forty-five female convicts, at which Lord ——— had been present on Friday. He could hardly refrain from tears in speaking of it. He called it the deepest tragedy he had ever witnessed. She read and expounded the Scripture with almost miraculous effect.'

I see her in the condemned cell with the poor wretches who, on the morrow, will become the prey of the gallows; I see her on the deck of the convict ship that is about to bear its living freight of human misery to the uttermost ends of the earth; I see her in hospital wards; I see her in lunatic asylums; I see her on battleships; I see her in the committee-rooms of the House of Lords and the House of Commons; and I see her, very frequently, in the palaces of kings. The last pages of her biography are almost entirely concerned with her pilgrimage from Court to Court on behalf of the unfortunates who languished in cells and dungeons.

VI

But Elizabeth Fry's *text?* What was the message
that reduced the gay young girl to sudden tears as,
wearing her purple shoes with scarlet laces, she sat
listening to the American Quaker? What was the
passage with which she herself played, like a skilful
musician, on the memories and emotions of the most
callous and abandoned reprobates? On that point
there can be no doubt at all. At a drawing-room
meeting held in the house of Sir Thomas Fowell
Buxton, the Rev. Daniel Wilson (afterwards Bishop
of Calcutta) asked Mrs. Fry whether any particular
passage of Scripture had proved specially useful in
dealing with criminals lying under sentence of death.

'I can have no hesitation in answering thy question,' replied Mrs. Fry; 'one passage I have found
far more effectual than any other. I refer to the
story of *the Woman which was a Sinner* in the latter
part of the seventh chapter of Luke's Gospel. The
simple reading of that story has softened the stoniest
hearts, and made eyes weep that never wept before.'

On one of her last visits to France, I find her addressing the inmates of the old prison at Nismes.
'She began in the most touching tone of voice on the
conversion of the woman of the city, who was a
sinner; her loving much because forgiven much; her
washing her Lord's feet with her tears and wiping
them with the hairs of her head. She spoke in a
strain of awful entreaty to the hardened and pro-

fane. The listening expression of all countenances showed how deeply her words impressed them. Many tears were shed, and she heard afterwards that, among these hopeless men, instances of real repentance and amendment of life had occurred.'

This story—the story of *the Woman which was a Sinner*—was, Mrs. King Lewis tells us, Mrs. Fry's favorite theme. She was speaking on it, 'in those sweet, silvery tones of hers,' when Thomas Carlyle heard her. 'It went from her heart to the inmost heart of her hearers,' he says. And she herself has told that she never read that great story of divine compassion and forgiveness without feeling her faith fortified and her affection for her Lord inflamed.

VII

Her tireless labors—domestic and public—wore down her strength at last. When she was a bright young girl—the Betsy of the purple shoes—an aged Quaker, Deborah Darby, was moved to prophesy of her that she would be a light to the blind, speech to the dumb, and feet to the lame. The prophecy had been nobly fulfilled. The dread of death that had always clouded her mind gradually lifted. 'I am ready now,' she said, 'to see the King in His beauty!'

> . . . So when her hour
> Had come, her children round her, she prepared
> To meet the Lord she loved. She, whose long life

Was lived for Him; whose earliest waking thought
Was evermore for Him; whose gathering years
Were crowned with deeds of mercy; whose dear name,
In every clime, thousands of rescued souls
Uttered with tremulous lips, and full of praise;
Whose thought was always how to raise, to help
The poor, the sick, the fallen; how to strike
The fetters from the prisoner and the slave.

The words that had been the key-note of her life-work proved the comfort of her death-bed. 'The more I think of it,' she murmured, 'the more am I touched by the exquisite tenderness of the Saviour's ministrations—of His tone and manner to sinners!'

To the very last she sat adoringly at the feet of her Lord, anointing His feet with her tears and wiping them with the hairs of her head.

'I am nothing,' she exclaimed, 'nothing! I am poor, miserable, naked, helpless. I am *nothing,* but He is *everything,* but He is *everything*—my light, my life, my joy, my hope of glory. What should I be without Him?'

'O my dear Lord,' she prayed, with her last breath, 'help and keep Thy servant!' And on the wings of that prayer she who had lifted thousands from wretchedness to rejoicing entered triumphantly into the joy that knows no ending.

19

HEPSY GIPSY'S TEXT

Main character in *Hepsy, Gipsy* by Mrs. L. T. Meade.

Ephesians 3:19

I

HE that desireth the office of a novelist desireth a good thing, and earneth to himself a good degree. Mrs. L. T. Meade certainly has. *Hepsy, Gipsy,* is a tale of a hollow old oak and a tale of a hollow young heart. It is written to show that the hollow oak and the hollow heart are very much alike. In both cases there is the hoarded treasure; in both there is the sudden and desolating loss; in both there is the aching sense of emptiness; and in both there is the filling of the void with a greater and more enduring wealth. The hollow tree was the Druid oak. It stood in the depths of the great silent woods. No track led to it, and round about it the forest was thick with its dense growth of brushwood. A tangle of ivy clothed the decrepit old oak, completely concealing the yawning cavity, half way up the trunk, in which Giant Lee, the gipsy miser, kept his hoard of gold. Lee fancied that no one knew his secret, but there were two, at least, who shared it with him.

Hepsy knew all about it. Hepsy was the waif of the caravans. Nobody knew whose child she was,

and nobody cared. She was an odd little thing—
cracked, they said. Miss Joanna Baillie says that the
cracks in the brain of Shakespeare's Touchstone
were chinks that let in the light. The cracks in the
brain of poor little Hepsy certainly served the same
high ends. She seemed to know everything. She
knew the woods through and through. She was as
much at home in their deepest recesses as the linnets
and the squirrels. She knew just where to find the
choicest nuts and the brightest berries. How was
it possible for Giant Lee to have a hiding-place in
the woods for his hoarded gold without Hepsy knowing all about it?

And the thief must have known. I wonder how!
Very often, of an evening, the other gipsies would
entice Lee to the tavern and ply him with liberal
potations of gin in the hope that, in his drunken
garrulity, he would betray the secret of his hidden
hoard. Perhaps they succeeded. However that may
have been, one thing is certain. Hepsy was not the
only gipsy who knew where the miser kept his gold.

II

The hollow oak! And the hollow heart! The hollow heart was Hepsy's. She said so herself over
and over again. It was not always empty. There
was a time when, like the dark cavity in the gnarled
and ivy-mantled oak, it was stored with shining

treasure. Even as a tiny child, Hepsy was a dreamer of beautiful dreams. Her small head, with its tangle of raven hair, was filled with the quaintest and prettiest notions. She thought the strangest thoughts and said the oddest things. The other children of the caravan used to cluster about her, and she would tell them the most wonderful stories. For Hepsy heard in the woods voices that fell on no other ears; she saw in the sky things that no other eyes could see. She lived, Mrs. Meade says, in a queer, unknown, fantastic world of her own. 'No one could tell the marvellous tales that she could tell. As she warmed to her theme, she would raise her great, coal-black eyes and fix them on the sky, whilst her voice would rise and swell and her thin little form pant with excess of emotion. She conjured up scenes that were sometimes beautiful and sometimes dark and lurid. Her imagery was gathered from the sky and the sunset, from the brilliantly glittering stars and the cold moon, and from the deep, deep gloom of night as she had seen it in the thickest of the forest glades. All her stories were medley, confusion, nonsense; but they had the germs of genius in them, and they fascinated and sometimes even affrighted the gipsy people.' For some years this filmy treasure filled her mind and satisfied her heart. Unlike Giant Lee, she sometimes gave her wealth away. When Nancy, Lee's wife, lay dying, nobody could say a word to comfort her.

'I wish I knew where I were g'wine,' poor Nancy moaned again and again.

The women of the caravans appealed to her husband to help her.

'Say something to comfort her,' they urged. 'Gi' her a thought to die on. Anything!'

'I can't,' replied Lee. 'I ha' naught to say. She's a g'wine out, poor Nance is—she's a g'wine out like a bit of a flame when you stamp on it.'

'Oh, I wish I knew, I wish I knew,' sighed Nancy. 'I wish I knew where I was g'wine.' And at that moment Hepsy came to her help.

'I think there's a stairway somewhere,' she said, 'and you get up into the sunset. I don't know, but I think so; I'm allers looking for it. It's beautiful in the sunset. I think you'll go there, Nance!'

The gipsy women smiled to one another; but Hepsy didn't notice them; she just went on talking to the dying woman concerning the stairway, the golden stairway that led right up into the sunset. And Nancy died with a great light shining in her eyes.

It was only a pretty fancy. Like the filmy gossamer, irradiated by the sunlight and floating on the air, it was attached to nothing; it was supported by nothing; it had no foundation. But it pleased and quieted Nancy; and, since her pretty fancies charmed and satisfied those about her, Hepsy distributed her treasure with a lavish hand.

III

It was a dark and dreadful hour—the hour in which the gipsy discovered that the hole in the Druid oak was empty. It was none the less dark, and none the less dreadful, because, to other eyes, the hour was bright and sunlit. The soft beauty of that lovely Sunday morning mocked the black despair of the miser's heart. He had come at last to take the treasure from its hiding-place. He was breathless with excitement. A thrush was singing blithely on a bough near by; but he could only hear the thumping of his own heart. As he strode across the village green, plunged into the great tangle of bracken and undergrowth, and fought his way through the forest to the ivy-covered oak, he wiped from his brow the perspiration that his excitement had produced. He climbed the tree, thrust his hard hand through the thick belt of ivy and groped savagely in the hollow of the tree. It was empty! He bounded to the ground. 'A dark flush overspread his face; his eyes, which had looked gentle, bright, almost handsome, a moment before, now glowed with a ferocious, untamed glare. His treasure was gone! He forgot everything under the half-stupefying, half-maddening sense of loss which now overpowered him.' He staggered back to the gipsy encampment a changed man. The money that he had collected with such care, and loved with such devotion, was gone, gone, gone! The hole in the oak was empty! It was indeed a dark and dreadful day.

It was a dark and dreadful hour, too, in which Hepsy discovered the emptiness of her own heart. The sweet dreams of childhood are very flimsy; they will not stand the strain of the years. There came to Hepsy, as there come to all of us, difficulty and perplexity and sorrow and loss. The stern realities of life pressed upon her, and in the light of that experience, the pretty fancies of her girlhood seemed terribly frail. They would not stand the strain, and she abandoned them all. One day Ben—her most intimate acquaintance—happened to mention God.

'Who's God?' asked Hepsy.

'Oh, Hepsy!' exclaimed Ben, in astonishment.

'I don't believe in God,' muttered Hepsy in a dull, indifferent, despairing voice. 'There's no sunset and no stairway, and no God, nor nothing! I don't believe in nothing, Ben! There's a hole in my heart, and I wish I was dead. You feel awful hollow inside, Ben, when you has a hole in your heart!'

One of the gipsy women reminded Hepsy one day of the comfort that she gave the dying Nancy. 'I've often looked at the sunset since,' the woman said, 'and thought about the stairway leading into it, and wondered how you knowed.'

'I don't know,' cried Hepsy. 'I believe as it were a lie I told. I don't think as there's any stairway.'

'Oh, don't say that, Hepsy,' the woman pleaded.

'It's a pretty thought, and a bit o' comfort to catch on by. I often thinks of it, often and often!'

'No,' sobbed Hepsy, 'there's no sunset and no stairway nor anything. It was only a dream of mine!'

The hollow tree and the empty heart! The two voids were very much alike. Mrs. Meade says so. In describing the miser groping vainly for his treasure, she says that 'all was emptiness—the hole in the tree was a little deserted chamber, as hollow and void as was poor Hepsy's starved heart at that moment. The treasure had taken to itself wings.'

The gold had gone! Poor Giant Lee!

The heart was empty! Poor Hepsy!

IV

And, of the two, Hepsy's loss was the greater. In this world of intensely pathetic things, few things are more pathetic than the utter desolation that, sooner or later, they experience who look into their own hearts and find them empty. Viscount Amberley and Professor Clifford were among those who, in the rough and tumble of strenuous days, lost the faith of their childhood. 'Candor compels me to admit,' wrote Lord Amberley, long afterwards, 'candor compels me to admit that, in giving up the faith of my young days, I have relinquished a balm for a wounded spirit for which it would be hard to find an equivalent in all the repertories of science and in all the treasures of philosophy.' And Professor Clifford, describing his scepticism, says that he has seen the spring sun shine out of an empty heaven, and has felt with utter loneliness that the Great Companion was dead. 'I am not ashamed,' says yet another, 'to confess that, with the denial of God, the universe has lost for me its soul of loveliness; and when at times I think, as think at times I must, of the appalling contrast between the hallowed glory of the creed which once was mine and the lonely mystery of existence as I now find it—at such times it will ever be impossible to avoid the sharpest pang of which my nature is susceptible.'

The sharpest pang of which one's nature is susceptible! Sharper, that is to say, than the pang that a man feels on discovering that his treasure is all stolen! In some touching verses, Francis Browne describes a band of pilgrims sitting by the sea-shore. They were talking of the losses with which they had met in the course of their lives:

> But when their tales were done,
> There spake among them one,
> A stranger seeming from all sorrow free:
> 'Sad losses have ye met,
> But mine is heavier yet,
> For a believing heart hath gone from me!'

> 'Alas!' those pilgrims said,
> 'For the living and the dead,

For fortune's cruelty and love's sore cross,
            For the wrecks of land and sea,
            But, howe'er it came to thee,
   Thine, stranger, is life's last and heaviest loss!'

That 'last and heaviest loss' was Hepsy's. The sudden anguish that the miser endured was terrible; but the constant aching of Hepsy's heart was sadder still.

V

Both the cavities were filled—the cavity in the hollow tree and the cavity in the empty heart. Indeed, the last chapter in the book is entitled *'Full!'*

When Nancy died, she bequeathed to her husband a baby boy. He never cared for it, and, but for Hepsy's constant mothering, the child could never have lived. But Hepsy made up her mind that Lee should care for the boy, and she compassed her end by guile. She knew—what did Hepsy not know? —that, on a certain day, Giant Lee was going to the Druid oak. Hepsy, with the baby, was there before him. When he reached the spot, he climbed the tree, and, in doing so, thought that he heard a strange sound in the heart of the oak. When he peered into the cavity, he was startled. For a very fair face; a face that was surrounded by an aureole of gold; a sweet, soft baby-face that seemed the very image of poor Nancy's, peeped out of the ivy and looked straight at him. And, in the end, Giant Lee took his neglected baby to his heart; and his boy was a greater comfort to him than all his gold could possibly have been.

And Hepsy? How was that empty heart of hers filled and satisfied? She one day heard a sweet voice singing:

> When I survey the wondrous cross
>   On which the Prince of Glory died,
> My richest gain I count but loss,
>   And pour contempt on all my pride.
>
> Were the whole realm of nature mine,
>   That were an offering far too small;
> Love so amazing, so divine,
>   Demands my soul, my life, my all.

'What's *"love so amazing"*?' Hepsy asked the singer.

And then, for the first time, Hepsy heard the story of *'the love of Christ that passeth knowledge.'* She listened to the story of the manger at Bethlehem, the story of the Garden of Gethsemane, the story of Calvary and its Cross. Poor Hepsy's empty heart drank it all in. She was thirsty for it. It was just what she wanted. It filled the aching void. It was the substance of which her stairway into the sunset was the shadow.

Later on, Hepsy rescued the baby from a blazing tent; and, in doing so, was herself terribly burned.

'But what's the pain?' she murmured, 'what's the pain? It's nothing when the heart's full; and my

heart is like a cup when you take it to the well and
fill it to the brim!'

'Love so amazing, so divine!'

'The love of Christ that passeth knowledge.'

It was for that love that all human hearts were
made; and no heart can be altogether restful and
altogether satisfied until, like an empty cup, it has
been filled to.overflowing at that divine fountain.

20

VICTOR HUGO'S TEXT
1802–1885
French poet, novelist, and dramatist.

1 Corinthians 13:13

I

THE birth of Victor Hugo was inauspicious. He seemed born but to disappoint! His parents had set their hearts upon a girl. They had even selected her name; and, in fond anticipation, they spoke familiarly of her as *Victorine.* At the birth of a boy they gasped in astonishment, and shortened the name to *Victor.* Victor! Playing on the name that was conferred in that hour of domestic discomfiture, Tennyson has made it seem, of all names, the most fitting:

> Victor in Drama!
> Victor in Romance!
> Cloud-weaver of phantasmal hopes and fears;
> French of the French and Lord of Human Tears!

The baby whose advent plunged his parents into embarrassment and confusion lived to be a peer of France, the storm-centre of a great political upheaval, and one of the most illustrious novelists of all time. Mr. Swinburne salutes him as the crowning glory of the nineteenth century, and, in all the ages, second only to Shakespeare.

There, then, he stands—'French of the French and Lord of Human Tears'! In his day everybody knew him. He was one of the most striking and picturesque figures of a stormy and eventful age. His contemporaries hailed him as a Man with a *Mission;* his successors salute him as a Man with a *Message.*

II

If Victor Hugo had been asked for his favorite text, he would not have hesitated for a moment. '*And now,*' he would have said, with characteristic and impressive emphasis, '*and now abideth Faith, Hope, Charity, these three; and the greatest of these is Charity.*' For those who have eyes to see, that text is inscribed on every page that Victor Hugo penned; it is the dynamic and the message of his life.

He was a man of simple *Faith.* He believed in God—in His Power, His Wisdom, His Goodness, His Love. He believed in the Bible. 'Let there be a Bible in every hut!' he pleads. He believed in the Saviour. 'Sow the villages with the gospel!' he cries. 'Jesus has something better to teach than Voltaire!'

He was a man of dauntless *Hope.* In his novels he portrays the foulest creatures imaginable, and shows that they may be uplifted and ennobled. 'The multitude can be sublimated,' he declares confidently. 'These bare feet, these naked arms, these rags, these shades of ignorance, these depths of abjectness, these abysses of gloom, may be employed in the conquest of the ideal. This lowly sand which you trample beneath your feet, if you cast it into the furnace, may become resplendent crystals; and, by means of the lenses that it makes, a Galileo and a Newton shall discover stars!'

And he was a man of invincible *Charity!* Mr. Stead used to say that *Les Misérables* is the supreme novel of Pity. 'It is,' he says, 'the very Gospel of Compassion, written by an Evangelist of Humanity. Here we have the wrongs of the wretched sung as never before by one who unites the tenderness of a Christian and the passion of a Revolutionist.'

Faith and Hope and Charity! And each of these abiding! '*Now abideth* ——' And not only aiding, but laboring—harnessed to beneficent and useful ends. For, with Paul and with Victor Hugo, Faith and Hope and Charity are no vapid sentiments; they apply themselves to human service. They are sternly and severely practical. In *The Lore of the Bee* there appears a legend of a poor woman whose hive was attacked by a pestilence. She was in great distress. At mass, on the following Sunday, the priest put the wafer on her tongue, but, instead of eating it, she took it home and slipped it into the hive. A few days afterwards she found that the disease had entirely disappeared; the wafer was in the centre of the hive; the bees had built around it a beautiful wax chapel with a lovely altar, on which the wafer lay; and they themselves were surrounding it, making a rhythmic and pleasing music, like a chant of praise. It is, of course, a myth; but in it a truth lies embedded. It is the truth that Victor Hugo lived to reveal. In each of his books he shows that, when religion is transferred from the abstract to the practical—from the cloister to the kitchen—miracles still happen. In each book he tells of unlovely lives made lovely by Faith and Hope and Love. Take, for example, *The Hunchback of Notre-Dame.* It is the most terrible of all his books; for our present purpose it is the least promising; yet see how the truth shines out!

III

In *The Hunchback of Notre-Dame* there are four outstanding characters—Quasimodo, the hunchback; Esmeralda, the dancing girl; Gudule, the recluse; and Claude Frollo, the priest. And each is redeemed, or partly redeemed, by that sublime Charity which, born of Faith and Hope, expresses itself in sacrificial service. Let us look first at Claude Frollo.

From infancy Claude has been destined for the Church. While quite a boy he was placed at the University. He has grown up on the missal and the lexicon. He has become grave, frigid, austere, steeped in the technique of theology and science.

One hot day a rumor reaches the University that the Rue Tirechappe is being devastated by the plague. Claude hurries home; finds that his parents are both dead, and that the only occupant of the house is his baby brother, crying in his cradle. He thus becomes an orphan and the head of a family at nineteen.

This [says Victor Hugo] was a crisis in the life of Claude. Hitherto he has lived only in learning; he now begins to live in life. He passes from reveries to realities. Moved with pity, he conceives a passionate fondness for his helpless infant brother. It is a strange and delicious thing, this human affection to one who has loved nothing but books. His baby brother makes a new man of Claude. He perceives that there is something in the world besides the speculations of the Sorbonne and the verses of Homer. He discovers that life without love is but a dry wheel, creaking and grating as it revolves. He abandons himself to the love of the little child with all the passion of his ardent, energetic, and concentrated character. This puny, frail, delicate creature—pretty, fair-haired, rosy, curly—moves him to the depths of his soul; and, grave thinker as he is, he begins to muse upon the child with feelings of infinite compassion. He is more than a brother to the infant; he becomes a mother to him.

It is thus that the Charity that is Love—the Love that is Charity—comes to Claude Frollo, imparting brightness and warmth to the spectral Faith and shadowy Hope that have shivered in his soul for years. Without Charity, Faith and Hope find existence difficult. This incident prepares the way for another.

About a year later, on a bright Sunday morning in 1467, a group of women are gathered in the stately porch of Notre-Dame, gazing with unutterable horror at a hideous monstrosity that has been placed in the wooden bed built into the wall. On this bed it is customary to expose foundlings to the public charity; any one takes them who feels so disposed. But this morning the women are scandalized at the creature on the bed. They draw each other's attention to his appalling ugliness.

He is, indeed, a monster of deformity. The poor little imp has a prodigious wart over his left eye; his head, covered with a forest of red hair, seems to jut out of his shapeless shoulders; his spine is crooked; his breastbone protrudes; and his legs are shockingly twisted. He is full of life, however, and his cry suggests unusual strength.

The women agree that it is disgraceful to expose such an atrocity in the church. But, all unseen, a tall young priest has been hovering in the background, listening. He is ashamed that, in the cold hearts of these fashionable worshippers, Pity has no place. Where is *Faith?* Where is *Hope?* And, above all, where is *Charity?* He strides towards the bed. The extreme ugliness of the creature only serves to intensify his compassion, and he vows in his heart that, for his baby brother's sake, he will be a father and protector to the unsightly little foundling. In the days that follow, tragic blemishes reveal themselves in the soul of Claude Frollo. Yet, all the while, there is a strain of nobleness in him. And everything that is high-minded, everything that is unselfish, everything that is good, can be traced back to those days when, at the call of an orphan and a hunchback, Charity crept shyly into that icy heart of his. So much for Claude Frollo!

IV

Esmeralda, the dancing girl, is the pearl of the book. She is only a waif, herding with the vilest of the vile in the foulest purlieus of Paris; yet her sweet simplicity, her maidenly purity, her dainty girlish beauty, protect her like a charm. She reminds us of those snow-white lilies that sometimes flourish amidst the grime and dust of a coal-mine. Yet her chief attraction lies neither in her stainless chastity nor in her artless beauty. If this were all, she would be nothing more than a pretty butterfly, flitting hither and thither across the pages of the book. But we all love Esmeralda because, in that dreadful hour in which poor Quasimodo writhes in excruciating anguish on the pillory, where he has been tortured for no other crime than the crime of his infirmities, it is the dancing-girl who dares the wrath of the mob and hastens to his relief. Quasimodo— whose deformities are accentuated by his half-naked and blood-stained condition—has endured for more than an hour the taunts and jeers of the crowd. His

face is purple: his eye glares widely; his mouth
foams with rage and agony; his tongue lolls out.

All at once he again struggles in his chains with an energy
of despair that shakes the whole machine; and, breaking the
silence which he has hitherto observed, he cries in hoarse
and furious voice, more like the yelp of a dog or the howl of a
wild beast than the articulate tones of a human tongue:
'Water!' This cry of distress, so far from exciting compassion,
serves only to amuse the loathsome rabble. They scream with
fiendish laughter. 'Water!' roars the panting Quasimodo.
At this moment he sees the populace make way. A young
female, fantastically dressed, approaches the pillory. She
is followed by a little white goat with gilt horns, and carries in
her hand a tambourine. Quasimodo's eye flashes fire. He
imagines that she, too, has come to mock him in his pain, and
to add her blow to the rest. He is choking with rage and hate.
If the lightning of his eye had possessed the power to blast
her, she would have been reduced to ashes. But, without
uttering a word she takes a flask from her girdle and applies
it to the lips of the exhausted wretch. Poor Quasimodo fixes
on her a look of unutterable woe and bursts into tears. Under
any circumstances it would have been a touching sight to see
this beautiful girl, so fresh, so pure, so charming, and at the
same time so weak, hastening to the relief of hideous deformity
in its dire distress. On the pillory, the sight is sublime. The
populace themselves are moved by it, clapping their hands
and shouting, 'Huzza! Huzza!'

Quasimodo never forgot that cup of cold water.
At the thought of it, he hazarded his life again and
again for Esmeralda's sake. Victor Hugo clearly
intended that cup of cold water as a symbol, a sacra-
ment. It is the visible representation of that divine
Charity which shed its hallowed lustre over Esme-

ralda's gentle life. There are times when, by a sacred process of transubstantiation, a cup of cold water becomes the Holy Grail.

V

And Quasimodo himself? In spite of his hideous ugliness, the hunchback is at times beautified, transformed, irradiated by three great loves.

(1) *He loves Notre-Dame.* From childhood he haunts its sacred precincts. Cut off from all other society, he dotes on the statues of the vast cathedral.

It is people with figures, made of marble, of kings, saints, bishops, who at least do not laugh in his face; they look upon him only with an air of tranquillity and benevolence. He therefore spends whole hours crouched before one of these images and holding solitary converse with it. If any one comes by, he runs off like a lover surprised in a serenade. Notre-Dame has been successively to him, as he has grown up and expanded, his egg, his nest, his home, his country, his universe. How he loves it!

(2) *He loves the Bells;* and, because he loves them so, Claude Frollo makes him the bell-ringer of Notre-Dame. Quasimodo gives each bell a pet name. He strokes them, he caresses them, he tells them softly of his fondness.

It is impossible to form a conception of his joy on the days of the great peals. He rushes up to the big bell—Marie, his best beloved—and pats her with his hand as you would do a good horse which you are going to put on his mettle. And when the peal begins, Quasimodo boils over with delight; he foams at the mouth; he paces excitedly to and fro; he vibrates with the music; he trembles in every nerve. All at once a frenzy seizes him; his look becomes wild; he watches the rocking bell as a spider watches a fly, and then, suddenly, flings himself upon it. Suspended over the awful abyss, he clings to the brazen monster by the earlets, yells at it in ecstasy, grinds his ugly teeth, spurs the bell with his heels, and struggles to impart to it his own fury. His red hair bristles up; his breast heaves and puffs like the bellows of a forge; his eye flashes fire; he forgets everything besides. At such a moment, the bell is no longer a bell; it is a dream, a whirlwind, a tempest, vertigo astride of uproar; a spirit riding a winged monster. The hunchback is mad—mad with love and joy!

(3) *And he loves Esmeralda!* Who can forget the day on which he so dramatically rescues her? She has been sentenced to death for witchcraft.

All at once, just as the executioner's assistants are preparing to obey the fatal order, the hunchback strides across the balustrade of Notre-Dame, seizes the rope with feet, knees, and hands, glides down the façade like a drop of rain down a pane of glass; runs up to the two men with the swiftness of a cat that has fallen from a roof; fells both of them to the ground with his enormous fists; bears off Esmeralda on one arm, as a girl would her doll, and, at one bound, he is in the church, holding her above his head and shouting with terrific voice: 'Sanctuary! Sanctuary!' It is all done with the swiftness of lightning.

Nor is it simply his mighty strength that is exhibited in this brave act. A wondrous wealth of tenderness appears. The Hunchback is changed beyond all recognition.

Palpitating all over, Esmeralda lies in his horny hands like a white drapery; but he carries her with infinite care. He feels that a thing so fragile, so exquisite, so precious, was not made for hands like his. At times he seems afraid to touch her, even with his breath. Then, all at once, he clasps her closely against this angular bosom, as his treasure, his darling, his all. No mother could have been more gentle. His Cyclops eye, bent fondly over her, gushes with a flood of tenderness, of pity, of grief. The women below are touched to tears; the crowd stamped with enthusiasm; for at this moment Quasimodo is really beautiful. Yes, he—the orphan, the foundling, the outcast, the hunchback—was, in this hour, fair to look upon!

With what touching delicacy he protects her during those sad days—the last days of her life—the days that she spends as his guest among the lofty turrets of Notre-Dame! He goes hungry that she may be fed. He gives her his poor bed, and, to guard her from the stealth of her foes, sleeps on the stones outside her door. No knight of romance ever behaved towards a fair lady in distress with more delicate chivalry. Quasimodo is a new creature. He is beautified by love—unselfish love— love in action—the love that expresses itself in sacrifice and service.

VI

And Gudule—the poor creature whose baby was stolen by the gipsies years ago—what of her? Gudule has shut herself up in her horrid cell with the one little pink shoe that the gipsies dropped in their flight. She has spent all the years cursing the gipsies in general and Esmeralda in particular, for she believes the dancing-girl to be of gipsy blood. But at last Esmeralda falls into the clutches of the pitiless old hag. The dancing-girl has only a few hours to live; but it looks as if Gudule will cheat the grim scaffold of its dainty prey by tearing the fair young creature to pieces in her cell. But, suddenly, Gudule finds something tied round her victim's neck. It is a little pink shoe—the companion to the one she herself has cherished through all the years! Esmeralda is her long-lost daughter!

What a scene is that which follows! The poor mother doting over her child—caressing her, fondling her, kissing her, bathing her in floods of tears, and then setting herself at any cost to save her! She fails. And, having failed, she lies at the foot of the scaffold, pleading to the last with her daughter's executioners. And thus mother and daughter, so long and cruelly separated, perish in the hour of reunion!

Yet nobody can read those last pages—the pages in which poor Gudule lavishes all the pent-up devotion of the lonely years on her newly found daughter —without feeling that Victor Hugo is still expounding his text.

When love comes back to the wretched recluse, she is no longer repulsive. When love comes back to Gudule, making her ready for any service and any sacrifice, the unhappy creature shines with a heavenly beauty and glows with an unexpected grandeur. All her latent womanhood and motherhood start to new and nobler life. When love comes back!

When love comes back! Life—even in its most sordid and squalid aspects—can be glorified by Love—Love serving and Love sacrificing. *'Now abideth Faith, Hope, Love, these three; and the greatest of these is Love.'* That—first and last, and all the time—is the message of Victor Hugo.

21

JOHN OWEN'S TEXT
1616–1683
English Puritan clergyman and author.

Psalm 130:4

I

THERE came to me, during my visit to the Homeland in 1924, many impressive and memorable experiences. One of them takes complete possession of
my mind to-day. It was a tranquil Sunday evening
in July. I had been invited to preach, morning and
evening, in John Wesley's old pulpit in City Road.
In my dread of arriving late, I had reached the spot
with half an hour to spare. I turned into the dreamy
and historic old cemetery immediately opposite the
church—the cemetery of Bunhill Fields. I had previously paid several pilgrimages to its honored
tombs, so that, on this occasion, wishing to be quiet
and unhurried, I resolved to concentrate on *two*.
Having stood for a few moments in reverent silence,
first beside the grave of *John Bunyan* and then
beside that of *John Owen,* I found a seat from which
I could restfully contemplate them *both*. In the
morning I had stood beside George Fox's grave, a
few yards distant in the one direction, and beside
John Wesley's, a few yards distant in the other.
And, the day before, I had been at Westminster

Abbey. To one who has spent most of his days in the uttermost ends of the earth, such experiences are almost overpowering. I sat there, that quiet summer's evening, glancing first at the tomb of Bunyan and then at that of Owen; and I understood, as I had never done before, the story of the dead Moabite who returned to life as soon as his body touched the bones of Elisha.

II

Again it is midsummer, and a Sunday. But I am in Australia, far from the tombs of the prophets. Yet, as I lounged this afternoon upon my sunlit lawn, a strange thing happened. I closed my eyes, and once more found myself on the seat in Bunhill Fields. And lo, as I sat there, John Bunyan came across the grass from the one direction, and John Owen from the other, and they both sat down beside me. They knew each other well. In the old days one was a travelling tinker, whilst the other was Vice-Chancellor of Oxford University. But what of that? They were of one heart and one mind, these two. Owen would walk for miles in the rain to hear Bunyan preach in a barn, and more than once stood for hours in the bleak wind of a winter's day listening to the words of grace that fell from the lips of the dreamer. The King rebuked him for his vulgar taste.

'I am astonished that you, the most scholarly man in the realm, should go to hear a tinker prate,' said Charles.

'May it please your Majesty,' Owen replied, 'I would cheerfully relinquish all my learning if I could acquire the tinker's ability for preaching!'

And it was as a result of Owen's earnest and persistent interposition that the hardships of Bunyan's imprisonment were mitigated and its period shortened.

And here they were, sitting together on the far end of my seat! With Bunyan's appearance we are all familiar. For that reason, it may be, it was the figure of Owen that enchained my attention. A gentle old man, of faultless attire and courtly bearing; a soft, melodious voice that gave a subtle impression of natural refinement and high culture; a face of singular gravity and sweetness, set off by a fine shock of long white hair—such was John Bunyan's companion. In his time he had been tall, stately, and majestic; but the years had reduced his stature, and much study had brought a stoop to the shoulders. His whole demeanor suggested a soul of rare delicacy and beauty. I fell in love with him at once. It was Bunyan, however, who spoke first.

'It was on a summer's evening like this,' he said, 'that one of my darkest distresses fell upon me. I had been under a great gloom for some days, but that evening it waxed worse and all hope seemed gone. I turned to the Scriptures, and, even as I opened the book, it was as if the clouds parted. And, as I was thus musing, I lit suddenly upon the words: *"There is forgiveness with Thee that Thou mayest be feared."* Those were good words to me that night. *"There is forgiveness!"* I said to myself. *"There is forgiveness!"* There is forgiveness with the Lord *that He may be feared!* That is, as I then understood it, that He may be loved and had in reverence. For the words seemed to me to show that the great God did set so high an esteem upon the love of His poor creatures that, rather than He would go without their love, He would pardon all their transgressions. Thus was my soul set at liberty.'

When I opened my eyes, I found *Grace Abounding* lying on the lawn beside me. And in it were these very words. But, with my eyes closed, they seemed to fall from the immortal dreamer's very lips. And, as he uttered them, the Vice-Chancellor sprang to his feet in delighted surprise, his fine eyes flashing with interest and sympathy.

'Why!' he exclaimed, with remarkable animation and intense fervor, 'it was by means of those very words that *my* dark soul was illumined. *"There is forgiveness with Thee that Thou mayest be feared"* —that sentence was the key that opened to me the gate of life. I was in depths inexpressible, and saw no way or means of deliverance; but God, by those

words, was graciously pleased to reveal Himself
unto me as a God pardoning iniquity, and I learned
to rest in His sovereign grace and plenteous redemption.'

When I opened my eyes, I found *The Works of
John Owen* spread out on the other side of my chair;
and there, in the sixth of these big black volumes, I
found these very words! But, with my eyes closed,
they seemed to fall from the lips of the great Puritan with that vigor and persuasiveness and charm
that enabled him to sway the hearts and probe the
consciences of his seventeenth-century congregations.

*'There is forgiveness with Thee that Thou mayest
be feared.'* That, most certainly, was *John Owen's
Text*. It captivated his heart; it dominated his ministry; it animated his life. We must look into the
matter a little more closely.

III

In the spiritual pilgrimage of John Owen there
are two profound and pivotal experiences. Whilst
still a student at Oxford, he became the victim of the
most gloomy apprehensions. Life and death seemed
equally intolerable to him. In the course of a visit
to London he was told that Dr. Edmund Calamy,
at Aldermanbury Chapel, was attracting multitudes
by his eloquence. The troubled young student re-

solved at any cost to hear him. He went, and, sitting in the pew, eagerly awaited the popular doctor's appearance. But he was doomed to disappointment. The vestry door opened, and a strange minister from a country parish entered the pulpit. Owen's companion suggested that they should leave the building and hurry away to hear some other popular preacher. But after his long walk to Aldermanbury, Owen was too tired for a further trudge. Instead, he bowed his head and prayed that it might please God, by the mouth of this unexpected preacher, to speak to his distressed condition. His prayer was heard; the preacher stated and answered the very doubts that had long perplexed his mind; and, by the time that the sermon was ended, he had begun to enjoy his first real experience of hope and peace. Strangely enough, although he afterwards exhausted every possible means of discovering the identity of the minister who, as he said, was 'the angel of God' to him that morning, he never succeeded in doing so.

The *second* experience came to him after he entered the ministry. The story is told by the Rev. Richard Davis, who eventually became the honored minister of a church at Rowel, Northamptonshire. When Mr. Davis was a young man he found himself under deep religious conviction. He felt that he ought to approach the Throne of Grace and throw himself on the divine mercy. But, before doing so, he sought an interview with Dr. Owen. In the course of conversation, the doctor startled him by asking an abrupt but pertinent question.

'Young man,' said the doctor, 'in what manner, may I ask, do you propose to go to God?'

'Through the Mediator, sir,' replied Mr. Davis.

'That is easily said,' answered the doctor, 'but I assure you that it is another thing to go to God through the Mediator than many, who lightly use that expression, are aware of. I myself was a preacher for some years, yet I had very little, if any, experimental acquaintance with access to God through Christ. Then, in His mercy, the Lord was pleased to visit me with sore affliction, whereby I was brought to the mouth of the grave, and under which my soul was oppressed with horror and darkness. But God graciously relieved my spirit by a powerful application of those precious words: *"There is forgiveness with Thee that Thou mayest be feared."* From that text I derived such encouragement, such peace, and such comfort, in drawing near to God through the Mediator, that the words have continued with me all through my ministry, and I have repeatedly preached from them with great delight.'

It was thus that John Owen became a new creature in Christ Jesus.

IV

In the days that followed, onerous responsibilities

fell upon him. At the age of thirty he preached before Parliament; the thanks of the House were conveyed to him by the Speaker, and the sermon was ordered to be printed. It was the first of many such experiences. By special command he preached the official sermon in connection with the execution of Charles the First. His handsome figure, his noble delivery, and his earnest style captivated the eye of Cromwell.

'Sir,' said the Protector, approaching him respectfully, 'you are a person whose friendship I much covet,' and, having spoken thus, he led him into the garden, and begged the preacher to become his private chaplain.

Owen's lot was cast in difficult times. He lived under each of the Stuarts; he held office under the Commonwealth; he passed through the fiery ordeal of the Civil War; he witnessed the Golden Age of Puritanism and sorrowfully watched its tragic collapse; he saw the Restoration; he saw London decimated by the Plague and destroyed by the Fire; and he saw the city rebuilt. Amidst these vast and dramatic changes I catch glimpses of him; now in earnest conversation with Cromwell at Whitehall; now discharging the important duties of his exalted office at Oxford, with youths like Christopher Wren, John Locke, and William Penn among his students; now discussing the perplexities of the times with Thomas Goodwin or Richard Baxter; and now strolling among the flower-beds of St. James's or along the Pantiles at Tunbridge Wells with Charles the Second and his brother, afterwards King James. But whether he is engrossed in private conversation, or in official correspondence, or in ministering to his people at Fordham or Coggeshall, or in preaching before Parliament, or in addressing his students, or in penning those cogent and powerful volumes that form his noblest monument, he never proceeds very far without making some reference to those golden words that, in the crisis of his spiritual experience, unlocked his prison door.

'There is forgiveness with Thee that Thou mayest be feared!' In one of these big black tomes lying on my lawn I find no fewer than two hundred and thirty pages dealing with this one text. Like an eager prospector crumbling every fragment of earth upon his claim in the expectation of seeing the glitter of gold, John Owen fondly examines the dotting of every *i* and the crossing of every *t,* lest some rich morsel of spiritual significance should escape him. He picks up each separate syllable, inspecting it from every conceivable viewpoint and in every possible light, as if it were a priceless gem having a hundred facets. Two hundred and thirty pages devoted to the elucidation of a single phrase! Is there any other book whose sentences could be submitted by a Vice-Chancellor of Oxford to so searching and exhaustive a scrutiny?

V

Strictly speaking, however, that monumental treatise of John Owen's on his text is not so much commentary as autobiography. 'It stands,' as the Rev. Andrew Thomson observes, in his *Life of Dr. Owen,* 'it stands intimately connected with the secret history of Owen's inner life; it conducts us through the turnings and windings along which he himself had wandered in the season of his spiritual distresses; and it shows us the way in which he at length found peace. He lays open his very heart and gives us a book which is instinct with the living experience of one who spake what he knew and testified what he had seen.' In the 'Introductory Note' at the beginning of these two hundred and thirty pages, and again at the very end, the doctor himself tells us as much. He has written this great work to show how God revealed Himself to his soul as a God pardoning iniquity, and how he came to rest in his Saviour's plenteous redemption.

There is the throb of genuine emotion in every paragraph. He seems to get excited as he opens up his text. Christie Murray used to poke fun at Charles Reade for hurling his sensations at his readers in capital letters. Reade seems to think that the tremendous shrill of those conspicuous sentences will take your breath away. Our Vice-Chancellor resorts to the same expedient. Where is forgiveness to be found? he asks. Nature knows nothing of it;

Conscience is equally ignorant; the Law reveals no hint of it; in Natural Religion the student finds no clue. But (and Dr. Owen prints the words in glorious capitals that seem like the expression of his ardor) *'THERE IS FORGIVENESS WITH THEE'!* With Thee! *With Thee! WITH THEE!*

'There is forgiveness with Thee that Thou mayest be feared.' We have already seen how Bunyan understood the words; John Owen interprets them very similarly. The two men may have talked the passage over; it is more than likely. *'There is forgiveness with Thee that Thou mayest be feared.'*

Feared! the doctor exclaims. What does the Psalmist mean by fear? He means a great *awe,* the doctor says on one page. He means a great *wonder,* he tells us on another. He means a great *admiration,* he explains on a third. He means a great *love,* he assures us later. And so on through two hundred and thirty pages. The fear that is produced by the divine forgiveness is the fear that casts out every other fear.

VI

In an age of civil strife, of violent upheavals, and of swift transitions, it was inevitable that the life of John Owen should be a chequered one. Like all the heroes of that tumultuous time, he had his exaltations and his abasements, his promotions and his degradations. But they came to an end at last. He was sixty-seven. He had retired from public life and sheltered himself in a quiet village which soothed his mind with a detachment and a peace which, he said, were almost as perfect as those that the grave would accord. On August 24, 1683, he was told that his work *On the Glory of Christ* had been published.

'I am glad to hear it,' he exclaimed, 'but oh, the long-wished-for day is come at last—the day on which I shall actually behold the glory of my Lord as I have never done before!'

And so, with eyes and hands exultantly uplifted, the most cultured of the Puritans shook the dust of earth from off him. His body was buried with reverence and great honor amidst the dreamy solitudes of Bunhill Fields. And, five years later, John Bunyan came up from Bedford and lay down to rest beside him.

22

WILLIAM TYNDALE'S TEXT

c. 1492–1536

English Bible translator and martyr.

1 John 4:19

I

How heartily and incredulously Harry Walsh would have laughed if some little bird had whispered in his ear that, in centuries to come, men would speak of William Tyndale as a grave and austere scholar, a stern and gloomy reformer, a severe and unbending controversialist! And Humphrey Monmouth would have felt very similarly. For Harry Walsh, a sunny little fellow of six, living at Old Sodbury, and Humphrey Monmouth, an alderman and well-known merchant of the city of London, knew Mr. Tyndale as one of the most winsome, one of the most genial, and one of the most lovable of men. Their happiest hours were spent in his society. Harry was the elder son of Sir John Walsh, a knight of Gloucestershire, and Mr. Tyndale was his private tutor. Here they are, sitting together beside a stile under a giant chestnut-tree, surveying from this green and graceful hillside the quaint little hamlet nestling in the hollow! Harry, in all the bravery of his trim velvet suit, with silk stockings and silver buckles, is perched on the top of the stile. His tutor, a young man of thirty, of well-knit frame and thoughtful but pleasant face, with nut-brown hair and deep-set hazel eyes, is seated on the footstep below him. A little brown squirrel eyes them suspiciously from a branch over-head, and a cuckoo is calling from the copse near by. Harry carries an armful of bluebells.

'What wonderful times we are living in!' exclaims Mr. Tyndale, his eyes sparkling with enthusiasm. 'Why, you and I ought to thank God every day, Harry, that He has sent us into the world just now! Every morning brings news of some fresh wonder!'

It was no exaggeration. The air literally tingled with sensation and romance. It was an age of thrills! The world was being made all over again. Civilization was being overhauled and recast. The very planet was assuming a fresh shape. One day Bartholomew Diaz added Africa to the map of the world; the next, Columbus added America; and then Vasco da Gama unveiled India to the eyes of Europe. Continents were springing up like mushrooms on a misty morning. And fresh continents produced fresh oceans. Twenty years after Columbus sailed across the Atlantic, Nunez de Balboa

> . . . with eagle eyes
> First stared at the Pacific—and all his men
> Looked at each other with a wild surmise—
> Silent, upon a peak in Darien.

Navigation was the fever of the hour. The vast oceans, so long a waste of loneliness, became a snowstorm of white sails. Every few days bronzed explorers seemed to be stepping from the decks of battered and weatherbeaten vessels to tell of new and astonishing discoveries in the Atlantic, in the Pacific, in the Indian Ocean—everywhere!

Nor was the land less sensational than the sea. For one thing, William Caxton was setting up his magic presses. Macaulay says that the invention of printing was the most notable event that took place during a thousand years of human history. It took the world by storm. Learned men, fashionable ladies, and great nobles thronged Caxton's little printing-house to see how the miracle was performed; whilst less intelligent people declined to go near it, declaring that such results could only be achieved by witchery, necromancy, and illicit commerce with evil spirits.

Moreover, to add to the wonder of it all, the printing-press came into the world at the very moment when the world had something worth printing. For it was the age of the Renaissance and the Reformation! Whilst Columbus was revealing a new world in the West, Copernicus was opening up a new universe in the skies, and Martin Luther was arousing a thousand thunders by tearing down the curtain that intervened between the common people and the Kingdom of Heaven. Faith's pilgrim path was being blazed. Astronomy was being born. Culture of all kinds was exciting boundless enthusiasm. Men were eager to think. In the realms of Religion, of Science, of Philosophy, of Music, of Art—indeed, in every department of learning—illustrious adventurers, whose names will live for ever, appeared like bright stars that twinkle suddenly out of the age-long dark. Men fell in love with the world—with this world and with every other. An infinite horizon was opened to the simplest minds. People who had lived in an age became citizens of all the ages. People who had lived in a tiny village found themselves exploring mighty continents. Lecky declares that the enlightenment and civilization of ancient times was restricted almost entirely to great centers like Athens and Rome; it never penetrated rural districts. In the awakening that took place in Tyndale's boyhood and youth it was quite otherwise. It was in those eventful days that mysteries that had for centuries baffled the minds of sages became the gossip of every chimney-corner and the talk of every tap-room.

'What wonderful times we are living in,' exclaims Mr. Tyndale, partly to himself and partly to his young charge perched on the rustic stile. Harry's golden hours are the hours that he spends rambling across the fields or through the woods in Mr. Tyndale's delightful company. For he knows that, as soon as they warm to their stride, his tutor will tell him the latest wonder of which the coach from London has brought word.

II

All things come to an end, however, as Harry discovers to his sorrow. As long as he lived he always declared that the deepest shadow that darkened his happy boyhood was his tutor's resignation. He never forgot the evening on which Mr. Tyndale told him that he must leave Old Sodbury.

The candles having been lit, Mr. Tyndale, as is his custom, reads to the two boys—Harry and Richard—a few verses from his Greek Testament, translating and commenting as he goes along.

'We must read our favorite verses to-night,' he had said, with a smile of singular sweetness in which, however, a suspicion of sadness seemed to linger. The boys know exactly the passage to which he refers. They know how dear to him are the verses that he has taught them, too, to love.

'*Ye are of God, little children,*' he begins, and reads on till he comes to the words: '*We love Him because He first loved us.*' Those words, he used to tell the boys, were the pearly gate through which he entered the Kingdom.

'I used to think,' he said, 'that salvation was not for me, since I did not love God; but those precious words showed me that God does not love us because we first loved Him. No, no; "*we love Him because He first loved us.*" It makes all the difference!'

The familiar passage having been read once more, Mr. Tyndale tells them that he is leaving them. The boys are soon in tears, and the tutor's gentle voice is husky.

'But why,' instantly demands Richard, breaking out in a passion of childish grief, 'why must you go?'

He draws them to him and attempts to explain.

'I must go,' he says quietly, with one arm round the shoulders of each boy, 'because I have found the work that God has sent me into the world to do. You have heard the things that have been said at dinner. Great and wise men, even preachers and prelates of the Church, come to dine with your father and mother, and say things that they could not possibly say if they knew aught of the Scriptures. If learned doctors and eloquent preachers are so ignorant of the divine Word, is it any wonder that *the people* are in darkness? A new day is dawning; the people are reading and thinking; it is time they had the Bible in their own tongue; and so, as I told your father and Dr. Hampton at dinner last night, I have resolved that, if God spare my life, I will cause every ploughboy in England to know the Scriptures better than the priests and prelates know them now. But it cannot be done here. I must go to London, and there, I trust, Bishop Tunstall will counsel and assist me.'

And so, after taking a sorrowful farewell of the household at Old Sodbury, Mr. Tyndale turns his face towards London.

III

But London receives him with a scowl. He soon discovers that he has poked his hand into a hornets' nest. On his first appearance at the palace, the bishop gives him the cold shoulder; and, when he persists in his overtures, he is threatened with all the thunderbolts that the Church can hurl. By every ship that glides up the Thames the writings of Martin Luther are being surreptitiously imported into England, and men are being hurried to prison and to death for reading them. There is nothing to indicate to the disappointed young tutor that, in centuries to come, his statue will hold a place of honor on the Victoria Embankment, and that, at its unveiling, princes and peers will bare their heads in reverence to his illustrious memory!

And yet, whilst Church and State frown upon his project and eye him with suspicion, those who come into intimate touch with him are captivated by his charm. From his old employer at Sodbury he brings letters of introduction to some of the merchant princes of the metropolis, and in their homes he soon becomes a loved and honored guest. With Alderman Humphrey Monmouth he stayed for more than six months. On week-days he worked quietly at his translation. 'But,' as an old chronicler says, 'when Sunday came, then went he to some merchant's house or other, whither came many other merchants, and unto them would he read some one parcel of

Scripture, the which proceeded so sweetly, gently and fruitfully from him that it was a heavenly comfort to the audience to hear him read the Scriptures. He particularly loved the writings of St. John.'

Harry and Richard Walsh must have smiled knowingly if that last sentence ever came under their notice: 'He particularly loved the writings of St. John.' They would see again the glowing face of their old tutor as he read the sentences that were so dear to him. And when he came to the words: *'We love Him because He first loved us,'* they would once more hear him tell of the way in which those priceless syllables had first impressed his soul.

Two things, however, are now clear. The *first* is that the people of England are hungry for the Word of God in their mother tongue; the *second* is that it is out of the question to attempt such a publication in London. This being so, he must brace himself for another painful wrench. Tearing himself from the homes in which so many delightful hours have been spent, he sets sail for the Continent.

IV

And, on the Continent, he knows of at least one kindred spirit. Martin Luther is hard at work translating the Scriptures. 'Would to God,' Luther cried, 'that this book were in every language and in every home.' Mr. Tyndale decides to hasten to Wittemberg and talk things over with the man who was shaking the very foundations of Europe. It is a pity that we have no classical painting of that historic meeting.

Luther and Tyndale! The German Bible of to-day is the most enduring and most glorious monument to Martin Luther; the English Bible of to-day is the most enduring and most glorious monument to William Tyndale! And here, in 1524, we see the two men spending a few memorable days together!

The rest of the story is well known. We have all chuckled over the way in which Tyndale outwitted his old antagonist, the Bishop of London. The New Testament in English is at last complete. 'It is called the *New Testament*,' Tyndale explains, 'because it is the Last Will of Jesus Christ, in which He bequeaths all His goods to those that repent and believe.' But how is it to reach England? The ports are closed against it! The book is contraband! Yet, in crates and casks and cases, in boxes and barrels and bales, in rolls of cloth and sacks of flour and bundles of merchandise, the Testaments come pouring into the country!

'Very well!' retorts the bishop, 'if we cannot *ban* the books, we'll *buy* the books and *burn* them!' He does so, only to discover, as soon as the flames of his famous fire have died down, that, in buying them, he has provided Tyndale with the wherewithal to print a larger and better edition!

We have all experienced the thrill of this brave, adventurous career. He was harassed; he was ex- communicated; he was driven from pillar to post; he was hunted from country to country; he was ship- wrecked; he was betrayed; he was imprisoned; he was tortured; and, at last, he was sentenced to a shameful death.

And we have all felt the pathos of that last letter of his. He is only fifty-six; but he is worn out and decrepit. Lying in his damp cell at Vilvorde, await- ing the stroke that is to emancipate his soul for ever, he reminds his friends that the date of his execution has not been fixed and that winter is coming on. 'Bring me,' he begs, 'a warmer cap, something to patch my leggings, a woollen shirt, and, *above all, my Hebrew Bible!*'

'*Above all, my Bible!*'

The words are eminently characteristic. He lived for the Bible; he died for the Bible; and he mounted the scaffold knowing that the Bible was being read in every chimney-corner, on every village green, and in every tavern and coffee-house in England.

V

It is a sharp October morning in 1536. The young squire of Old Sodbury—Henry Walsh—sits by his dining-room fire with his hands in his pockets and a far-away look in his eye. His handsome young wife, entering the room, demands the cause of his unwonted abstraction.   Drawing her to him, he tells her that news has just reached the village that his dear old tutor, William Tyndale, has been strangled and burned for his faith.   Then, gently taking her arm, he leads her across the room, and they stand for a moment in reverent silence before the text upon the wall:

*WE   LOVE   HIM   BECAUSE   HE   FIRST
LOVED US.*

He does not repeat the story; she has heard it from his lips so often.

.   .   .   .

And so our studies complete their circuit.   For with this text we began.   It was *William Law's Text;* it was *William Tyndale's Text;* it is the text of all those whose hearts have made response to the Love that Aches Hungrily until it is Requited.